# Higher Education: Significant and Contemporary Concerns

INFO-TEC, Inc. • Cleveland, Ohio

To Order:

INFO-TEC, Inc.
P.O. Box 40092
Cleveland, Ohio 44140
(216) 835-1610

# CONTENTS

# PREFACE

Within the dynamic environment of institutions of higher education, there exists a perpetual need to share information concerning contemporary ideas and activities. These ideas and activities change from year to year and decade to decade, however, there remains the certainty of change and the examination of new ideas that is inevitable.

This publication examines in some detail several significant contemporary activities whose visibility and concern call for analysis by institutions of higher education. As we near the end of the decade of the 1980s and enter the decade of the 1990s, colleges and universities will have reached the point of stabilization of enrollments and maturity of fledgling two-year colleges. This publication is intended as a vehicle to assist academic administrators and faculty to a better understanding of their institution and its contemporary role. The contributors to this publication are varied in experience and background, however, are similar in their professional competence and achievements.

In Chapter One, **Ray Sanchez** discusses in a frank and effective essay the institutional responsibilities in the education of culturally different students. He discusses the culture and its impact on learning behavior of all students, traditional as well as culturally different. He raises to the point of visibility the problems imposed upon instructors due to the standards and values that may have been established, versus the real world of the culturally different student. Mr. Sanchez examines the impacting factors including: language proficiency, textbook treatment of minority contributions, economic isolation, traditional perceptions, and professional under-representation of different values. He also makes visible the need for faculty to be cognizant of the problems of the physically handicapped.

He provides self-help tips for adjunct faculty as well as departmental concerns to assist the institution in addressing the needs of culturally different students. He places special emphasis on students' concerns for class participation, an examination of "good" versus "rough" teachers, student accessibility to staff and general awareness of such overlooked factors as: name pronunciation, cultural holidays, flexibility, and utilization of internal resources.

In Chapter Two, **Ellison, Green** and **Smith** provide examination of a pressing contemporary concern — that of student retention. Their essay provides an examination of the nature of the student to be addressed in the "retention-dropout" problem. They discuss the causes of school discontinuation and the related cost impact to the institution because of school dropouts. An examination of the open access versus student retention paradox is presented. Considerable effort is addressed to issues related to student retention, i.e. the dropout versus intermittent student, information available on student retention and using information for effective student retention programming. They present a model to address the need for comprehensive student retention programs including assessment programs, as well as the importance of organizing an effective retention program. Within this context a model organizational structure is presented with elements of a comprehensive plan including: centralization, integration and modification of present efforts, a data collection mechanism, and definition of goals. Finally suggestions for strategies addressing the student drop-out problem are presented including: orientation, financial assistance, a sense of community, academic excellence, other direct assistance, special student group retention, high risk students, former students, and returning students. Finally an evaluation of student retention programs and a student retention case study is presented.

In Chapter Three, **Al Smith** takes an in-depth look at the total approach and concepts of faculty evaluation. Although initially many of his precepts where devoted to adjunct faculty, the application of his findings may be directed to all college staff. He commences with proposed conceptual schemes for evaluation, including a model containing the broader view of such evaluation and the performance contract. In a framework for faculty evaluation he outlines the survey and case study of the Southern Regional Educational Board with the identification of related concepts. He also addresses in the framework for staff evaluation criteria and standards.

An extensive discussion is presented outlining a 14 step strategy for success in faculty evaluation. Within the strategy he discusses preliminary activities and support necessary; factors that help unhinder the process; and strategies for implementation. Also covered is the testing, implementation and evaluation of the process. A summary is given outlining the lessons learned in the process emphasizing the importance of goal setting and compromising between faculty and administration. Finally, a list of conclusions as a guide for comprehensive plan is presented.

In Chapter Four, **Donnelly** and **Poole** discuss the evolution of the continuing education movement — a comparatively recent event on the higher education scene. Significant discussion is given concerning the continuing education budget and its impact on the institution as well as the impact on curriculum, faculty, and community. A revelation of positive, negative, and pragmatic outcomes is presented. They establish, describe and define the variations of continuing education programs presented at different types of institutions. Within this context observations for developing continuing educational packaging are made.

An analysis of the institutional reasons for entering

continuing education endeavors is presented with observations concerning revenues versus service as the end product. In analyzing factors related to successful development of continuing education programs, a discussion includes such factors as: time, space, faculty, and administration. The importance of analyzing the continuing education program in light of the college mission and the administrative commitment is reviewed.

In Chapter Five, **Audni Miller-Beach** addresses the topic of faculty renewal during a period of minimum faculty mobility. The chapter analyzes the need for faculty renewal, the process of renewal and the sources of renewal. Dr. Beach points to the need for renewal to accommodate change, accountability for faculty and the influx of new clientele, in addition to new technologies. Several very interesting case studies include the discussion of: family relationships, students as a source of meaning, relationships with colleagues, and work as a source of meaning. In conclusion Dr. Beach outlines events associated with renewal, work and renewal, relationships and renewal and creating an institutional climate for renewal.

—Donald Greive, Ed.D.

*Dedicated*
*to*
*the memory*
*of*
*Jeff & Jessica*

# Teaching Culturally Different Students in Higher Education: A Practical Guide for College Faculty

Ray Sanchez

Since the social revolution of the 1960s, a larger number of American college students have come from the ranks of the culturally — and racially — different strata of our society.[1] And, although the percentage of minority students who actually graduate is relatively small,[2] their presence and their

Ray Sanchez is former Dean of Extended Services previously the Evening Division of San Antonio College in San Antonio, Texas. As Dean he served approximately 10,000 part-time evening students. He holds both his B.A. and M.A. from St. Mary's University in the same city. A sixteen-year veteran of the part-time faculty at S.A.C., Mr. Sanchez has served as Director of a community based Educational Talent Search Program as well as Director of a Special Services to Disadvantaged Students Project co-sponsored by two local universities.

Long active in educational circles dealing with minority issues, Mr. Sanchez served five years as a member of the city's Library Board and as its chairman during his last year and a half. He has served eleven consecutive years as a member of the Bexar County Historical Commission. Mr. Sanchez has been legally blind since 1969.

needs have posed an educational challenge college instructors often feel ill-equipped to handle. College faculties have been and continue to be the ones most often faced with this challenge because of the "open door" policy coupled with the fact that many culturally different students come to college ill-equipped to overcome initially stringent admission requirements at four-year schools. Yet what I have to say applies to all levels of higher education. Who are considered culturally different students? What makes them different and from whom do they differ? What can you, as an instructor, do to help yourself in teaching this type of student? How can you help your students become better students?

## CULTURE

Before we attempt to provide answers to these questions we need to delve — at least in a rudimentary manner — into the question of culture. "Culture," writes H. Douglas Brown in his work on language learning, "might be defined as the ideas, customs, skills, arts, and tools which characterize a given group of people in a given period of time."[3] By its very nature, culture is learned human behavior which can be taught, as opposed to racial or genetic characteristics of an individual or group which are biologically *inherited*.

To put it another way, culture is learned human behavior and represents the sum total of attitudes and actions affecting many areas of an identifiable group including its art, language, religion, economics, history, politics, education and social patterns to a degree sufficient to render it distinguishable from another group or groups of human beings, since often some culturally different groups display some outward manifestations of their cultural and biological identity (*i.e.*, language, dress, skin color, etc.), care must be taken by an instructor not to assume that all members of a group share equally in all of the cultural characteristic of the group. A case in point is the fact that all Spanish-surnamed individuals do not necessarily speak or understand Spanish.

In the context of higher education, then, culturally different students appear to be those who because of factors reasonably beyond their control have been prevented from living, during their developing years, the experiences that would have prepared them for equal participation in the competitive process of American higher education.

Normally, this means that you will have culturally different students who have difficulty reading, writing, and understanding English; are experiencing varying degrees of isolation; have experienced discrimination and to some degree suffer or have suffered some of the physical and psychological handicaps discussed in the next few pages.

The number of factors impacting a culturally different group vary from group to group and are greatly influenced by the specific circumstance which produced a group's presence in this country. Culturally different does not always equate with the term "immigrant" in the traditional sense. For example, American Indians were here to greet the Europeans when they arrived; Black Americans were forced to come to America; and Mexican Americans had settled the Southwest and Florida 300 years before the waves of immigrants from the United States crossed the Mississippi River. Again, a traditional perception and role for women has cut across cultural and racial boundaries of the western world for centuries.

## STANDARDS VS. VALUES

In terms of college performance many of the "standards" which establish the norm for performance are traditionally set by individuals who share a white, male, Anglo-Saxon, Protestant view-point. This is all well and good. The problem for you as an instructor occurs when the values and standards of your students clash. This occurs because culturally different students are just that, namely *different*. Obviously the greater the degree of difference, and the greater the degree of difficulty a student has in adjusting to the difference, the less probability of success in American higher education. This is the essence of the concept of "cultural shock" as advanced by John H. Schumann of the University of California at Los Angeles.[4]

The factors listed below are applicable to a vast majority of culturally different students in the United States. The items are not new and certainly have been the focal point of concern by educators for at least the past 25 years. In this treatment, specific application of the factors is often made to one group of culturally different students, the Mexican American (not the Hispanic).[5] This application is for purposes of illustration and certainly not to establish or reinforce a stereotype. At the same time, it will provide the reader with some insights into a sub-group of the Hispanic community.[6] Other culturally different groups certainly share the impact of the seven factors to a greater or lesser degree. It is expected that the treatment presented in this chapter plus the bibliography and recommended readings will set the stage for you to adapt your teaching so as to allow for most culturally different students in your region. Conversely, your students need to be made aware of how the values of the American system may differ from their values. This will allow them to understand what is expected of them in the classroom and why. So long as this process is not judgmental it can help the educational process greatly. If you have been teaching any length of time some of the items discussed in the following section are already evident to you. The reasons — theoretical or empirical may not be as evident.

## THE IMPACTING FACTORS

1. *English Language Proficiency.* Competent command of
   English as the prime tool of American higher education is a
   must for scholastic success. Lack of competence — and I
   exclude accent as a factor of true competence — affects all
   aspects of college work. But failure to achieve competence
   may often be affected by one or more of the eight items
   under discussion. For example, not withstanding the fact
   that a large percentage of Americans lack adequate
   command of English, an undetermined number of Mexican
   Americans may subconsciously resent English for
   historical reasons which have placed us in the position of a
   colonized people within our own country.[7] This resentment
   has been compounded by the traditional lack of
   appreciation on the part of most Americans for other
   languages best (or worse) exemplified by the "Americans
   speak English" syndrome.

2. *Inadequate Treatment of A Group's Historical
   Contribution In Textbooks.* Although much progress has
   occurred in recent years, far too many textbooks in
   American History are still being published which fail to
   provide adequate treatment of minority contributions to
   the development of the United States. When a text glosses
   over the history of Spanish America west of the Mississippi
   (1519-1848) in a few pages, Mexican American students
   must conclude that this aspect of American history was of
   no consequence. The fact the conclusion is erroneous and
   either conscious or subconscious in no way diminishes its
   negative impact on the self-image of the student.

3. *Economic Isolation.* Poverty impedes education. Taken for
   granted educational support systems such as
   encyclopedias, dictionaries, and now, home computers are
   absent from economically deprived homes. Also missing
   from the student's home environment are college trained
   parents, grandparents, and other relatives. Many

culturally different students fall into this economic isolation which fails to prepare them for educational success.

4. *Traditional Perceptions.* Many members of American society still cling to regressive and traditional perceptions about culturally (and racially) different peoples and about their history, language, ability and "place" within the American "way of life."[8] Guilty of this myopic view are some of our colleges which view some culturally different groups *in toto* as scholastically incapable and "not college material."

5. *Professional Under-Representation.* The under-representation — and at times deliberate exclusion — of culturally different group members from American higher education often is cited as "proof" to the community at large that group "x" or group "y" simply "can't cut it" in order to make it through a graduate program. Legitimate academic practices such as screening committees, tenure, and governance are at times subverted to limit access to faculty and administrative ranks. The number of culturally different applicants who do manage to filter through are too few or too intimidated to provide an effective challenge to the system. The culturally different student is thus denied access to role models who automatically share a common base of experience and who still may share his/her viewpoint.

6. *Different Values.* Even though much already has been written and alluded to about different values earlier in this chapter, the subject merits addressing independently as an impacting factor. Incongruent codes of cultural group ethics which may view ambition, competition, cooperation, wealth, religion, family, ethnicity, race and even education itself with varying degrees of difference from the "norm" certainly produce a trauma for the student who has not learned to acculturate or is functioning as a "cultural

schizophrenic".[9] For the student who is truly bi-cultural, the ability to shift from the value system of his home culture to the value system of the dominant culture becomes almost automatic, although trauma must undoubtedly occur.

7. *Internal And External Political History Of A Group.* The political relations of the United States with a culturally different group or its country of origin affects students from the group. This is uniquely true of American Indian, Black and Mexican American students. For example, in its western expansion to the Pacific, the United States fought wars of annihilation against many Indian nations. These wars ended when the survivors were confined to reservations.

Again, in its sweep through Florida and the Southwest, Americans resorted to infiltration tactics which joined "independence" movements in West Florida, Texas, and California in order to achieve territorial ambitions. This thrust peaked with the Mexican War at the end of which the United States annexed Texas and the present Southwest and California. The Hispanic survivors of that Manifest Destiny and their descendants were often dispoiled of their property and relegated to second-class citizenship.[10]

The American Black was ripped from his African womb and denied his name, religion, language, family — in short, his very essence — while being dispersed across foreign lands not of his own choosing. The only possession he was allowed to keep was his color.

In viewing the history of these three groups within the United States one might be tempted to wonder why events of three or four hundred years ago — or even 25 years ago — are still the focal point of resentments today. After all, the past *is* the past. True, except for the fact that we as a nation insist on justifying our record in a cloak of altruistic respectability. The vestiges of Manifest Destiny have

survived to the present day. Only the words have been
changed to obscure the concept. The frequently stated
cliche that we are *all* immigrants certainly ignores the
historical reality as it concerns the American Indian, the
Hispanic of the Southwest and the Black.

8. *Time Subtleties*. Another point that merits consideration is
differences in time perception and in counting clusters of
days. In terms of counting a week from today, Anglo-
Americans begin with tomorrow and count forward seven
days (thus excluding today as the first day in the sequence).
Mexican Americans and other Hispanics begin counting
with today and thus speak in terms of "eight days from
today" rather than seven days from tomorrow. The end
product could throw the whole count off by one day and
that could be devastating if a test is involved. Preferably
instructors should use exact dates in setting test dates to
avoid confusions.

## THE PHYSICALLY IMPAIRED MINORITY

Before closing this segment of my treatment I must add a
final group that needs consideration: the physically impaired,
cultural minority or not. Certainly, the subject deserves
treatment in a chapter of its own and I can make no claim of
expertise on the subject other than that gleaned from personal
experience. Yet the blind, the deaf, the crippled — in brief, those
hindered by infirmity from seeing, hearing, walking and
otherwise functioning in a physical setting tailored for the
majority already suffer a discrimination and isolation which is
unique to say the least. If they also happen to be culturally
different, they pose a double challenge to the college instructor.

## LEGACY IN THE CLASSROOM

The factors discussed so far either by themselves or in
combination have produced and are producing today groups of

students who will show up in your classroom at various stages of "cultural shock."[11]

Some of these students have recently arrived in the United States and are new to the culture shock experience. Others students may be lifelong Americans who encountered culture shock the first day of the first grade and who are still in a culturally transient state. Some in your class who might appear to be culturally different (because of their physical characteristics) will be totally mainstream.

## WHAT YOU CAN DO TO HELP YOURSELF

Given the preceding discussion, here are some nuts and bolts suggestions that may be of help. Many of these thoughts probably popped into your mind while reading the chapter and may appear obvious. But seeing them in print (as a checklist) may help you further crystalize your plan of action.

1. Self-analyze your own perceptions about culturally different and physically impaired groups within your community and your immediate teaching environment. Be totally frank and honest about the facts you know; your feelings; your biases.

2. Study and reflect upon how the eight factors discussed in this chapter have impacted your community at your college. Do you observe other factors not included in the eight but equally impacting your particular setting?

   Look around you. Ask your college E.E.O. Office about employment patterns; become familiar with local and state history. Do economic cleavages parallel cultural groupings? Do certain cultural or physically impaired groups account for a large percentage of your college trained or your school dropouts?

3. Examine your textbooks and other instructional materials. Re-examine your notes and handouts. Do these materials perpetuate negativism and cultural insensitivity?

4. Read your tests. Are these constructed in a manner or style that caters only to students from college prep high schools? This is an especially important element in community college teaching. Are questions phrased with an unnecessary degree of subtleness which subconsciously penalizes those whose first language is not English?

## WHAT YOU CAN DO
## ABOUT YOUR DEPARTMENT

1. How do your peers perceive culturally different and physically impaired students in the context of higher education?
2. Does your department reflect some kind of cultural mix? Are your colleagues aware of the general background of culturally different students at your institution of higher learning? Do professional development programs address such topics as retention, teaching the ill-prepared, and teaching the culturally different and physically impaired student?
3. Do your textbook selection practices ignore the issue of superficial treatment of minority contribution to history, literature, science, and other disciplines? Are monies budgeted to purchase supplemental materials to fill such gaps? If so, are these materials bought? And, if bought, are the materials used as part of the standard curriculum by everyone? Or, one may regretably ask, is bigotry or calloused insensitivity hiding behind "academic freedom"?

## WHAT YOU CAN DO ABOUT YOUR
## STUDENTS — ALL YOUR STUDENTS

The answer to the questions below should provide you with a clue to your teaching techniques and how appropriate these are to your student needs, background, and general orientation. If you conclude they are not, what alternatives might be suitable?

1. Do you rely exclusively on pencil and paper tests? Do not be afraid to note conversations on subject matter over coffee or individual conferences. Note also class participation. After all, we make judgments about people we come in contact with daily on non-paper and pencil factors. Go ahead and be "subjective" about your students' comprehension and grasp of a subject.

2. Do you have a high dropout rate and are culturally and physically different students over-represented in this area. Why?

3. Are you considered a "good" teacher or a "rough" teacher? Some teachers confuse their role with that of a drill sergeant. The two are not necessarily synonymous.

4. Are you accessible either in person or by the telephone? Do you insist that students in academic difficulty come to you instead of you approaching them?

5. Are your students allowed to "interrupt" your lecture with questions? Does this visibly annoy you?

6. Are you in the classroom "to get through the book" or to teach your students? This is an especially sensitive topic with community college instructors who must teach introductory courses. My suggestion is that you structure your course to include no more than one or two subject areas where you cover the topic "in depth" as you would an upper division class. This will provide you with something to look forward to and perhaps challenge the interest of your students.

7. Do you butcher family names and make no effort to learn the phonics of Hispanic, Oriental, Middle Eastern or other names which may pose us Americans difficulty?

8. Are you unaware or even unsympathetic to cultural or religious holidays other than your own? For example, among Mexican Americans the following are among the

very significant cultural holidays traditionally honored:
*Cinco de Mayo* (5th of May, 1862). Commemorates the
successful battle against 6,000 superior French troops.
Leader of the Mexican defenders of the city of Puebla was
Texan-born General Ignacio Zaragoa.

*Diez y Seis de Septiembre* (16th of September, 1810).
Recalls when Fr. Migual Hidalgo y Costilla declared the
political independence of New Spain (Mexico) from the
mother country. The present Southwestern United States
was part of New Spain and two insurrections (1811, 1813)
sprang up in Texas to support the Hidalgo effort.

*Dia de la Hispanidad* (Hispanic Day, October 12, 1492).
Celebrates the discovery of the Americas by Christopher
Columbus. This is an important date for all Hispanics.

*Dia de la Virgen de Guadalupe* (Day of the Virgin of
Guadalupe, December 12, 1531). Honors the several
apparitions of the Virgin Mary to Aztec Indian Juan Diego
asking that a church be built on Tepeyac Hill near Mexico
City.

*Las Posandas.* Reenacts the search for shelter by Joseph
and Mary in Bethlehem. Traditionally a celebration
conducted on each of the nine nights before Christmas, this
ritual dates back 400 years.

9. Do you feel some culturally and physically impaired groups
   are just not "college material"? You may be correct. Some
   groups — especially at the underclassman level — may not
   be college material at the stage of educational development
   they find themselves at that moment. They may have to be
   viewed as the raw material which can be refined given the
   right motivation into the professionals and technicians of
   tomorrow. They are your challenges and you are theirs.

10. Do you provide alternatives for your working students
    (especially night students) in lieu of reading books on
    library reserve or attending other functions for extra credit
    or as a normal part of the class?

## SOME SPECIFIC TECHNIQUES

1. Approach your students where they are academically, not where they ought to be. Then work towards the level where they ought to be. This is a particularly useful approach in community colleges and in departments where the grade of "IP." (In Process) is used. IP. allows a student to repeat a course without experiencing a punitive grade. If IP. grades are not used in your institution/department find out why not and encourage their use.

2. Assume that your culturally different students want to play by the rules while retaining much of their heritage. However, be equally certain that you are not demanding equal performance for "equal performance sake" from your physically different students when you could obtain the same results employing other methods. Contrary to popular insistence, some physically different individuals have to be treated differently because they simply must be. So long as the results are the same it does not matter. Whenever possible, think of alternatives.

3. Send them to the Counseling Department for general academic direction but do not expect everything to automatically improve in your class overnight. Remember, the counseling staff is not sitting in your classroom. Only you can provide specific direction on what you expect of your class and how to achieve it. You may not be a "counselor" but you certainly are an "advisor."

4. Use very concrete and familiar examples in your instruction. Generally culturally different students appear to have some difficulty handling abstractions.

5. Encourage students to ask questions "on the spot." A student with an unresolved question will cease to absorb new information. Depart from your prepared lecture until all relevant questions are resolved.

6. Give your class plenty of relevant handouts. Due to my

partial vision, I perhaps do too much in this regard. But, also, I find I can hold each student accountable for reading any items if I have given him or her a copy. This also encourages night students, nearly all of whom work and have limited time to make extra trips to the library. However, watch out for violations of copyright laws by clearing any mass duplication with your library or Learning Resources staff.

In regards to outlines, be sure to stress that these are just that outlines. Culturally and physically different students — not to mention the rest — weaned on easier to grade "objective" tests need to be shown how to fill-in detailed notes or specifics.

7. Go over essay test questions to ensure everyone understands what you expect in terms of answers.

8. Allow and encourage the use of dictionaries during tests. In real life situations you are expected to consult a dictionary when in doubt on the spelling of a word. It makes little sense not to allow their use during your tests.

   The time a student spends agonizing over spelling could be better spent improving content and with less anxiety. What is true of the use of a dictionary is also true concerning the use of a Thesaurus.

9. Allocate more time for tests than you feel necessary. Some students — regardless of background — are poor at taking tests. Allow them to bring in a snack or soft drink to have during the test. Suggest a jacket or sweater to help those who are cold natured. Set the stage by relating a humourous anecdote or two. All these things will help relieve anxiety and tend those apt to "freeze" when being tested.

10. When you return your first major test, dismiss the class early enough to allow you about an hour for individual conferences with students who did poorly. See them in complete privacy. Ask questions regarding their general

academic peformance in high school and other college courses; their major; their "best" and "worst" subjects; if they are working too many hours; the amount of hours they studied; why they think they did poorly, etc., etc. Ask to see their notes also.

11. Get rid of the frame of mind which dictates that you must have a certain percentage of "A's," "B's," etc. Remember, the Bell curve was intended to evaluate the performance of students from the same academic training, college background, culture, etc., etc.

12. Give your students "practice" quizzes for non-credit to acclimate them to your individual style of testing.

13. Have all your students read aloud during the first two class sessions so you can evaluate their individual level of comprehension.

## CONCLUSION

The task of responding to the educational needs of culturally and physically different students rests equally on the shoulders of the institution, the department and each member of the faculty and administration. If your voice as an instructor is one of a very few which can be heard expressing concern on the subject, then your task is difficult indeed. Yet difficult or easy, it appears to me that professional ethics requires that success or failure by any student in your class should be based upon a performance unobstructed by irrational factors such as we have discussed. To be sure, even in the most ideally unobstructed teaching/learning environment some students will still fail. So it must be. But in no instance should an instructor's lack of sensitivity ever surface as a probable cause.

## FOOTNOTES

(1) For example, while the total number of college students increased 34.8% in the decade from 1972-1982, the number of Black and other races increased 85.3% and of women 60.8%. Reatha Clark King, "The Changing Student," *National Forum,* Phi Kappa Phi Journal, Summer, (1985), p. 23.

(2) Blacks, Hispanics, Asians or Pacific Islanders cumulatively accounted for only 10.8% of the Bachelors Degrees and Blacks and Hispanics for 8% of the Masters Degrees awarded in the 1980-81 school year. Candy L. Stoher, "Minority Progress", *School Products News,* July, (1985), p. 33.

(3) H. Douglas Brown, *Principles of Language Learning and Teaching,* (Englewood Cliffs: Prentice Hall Inc., 1980), p. 123.

(4) As defined by Schumann, cultural shock is "an anxiety resulting from the disorientation encountered upon entering a new culture". John H. Schumann, "The Acculturation Model for Second Language Aquisition," in *Second Language Aquisition and Foreign Language Teaching,* ed. Rosario C. Gingras, (Washington D. C.: Center for Applied Linguistics, 1978). p. 33.

(5) The term "Hispanic" encompasses individuals who share common roots of language, art, religion and other aspects of culture in a general way. Mexican Americans are a sub-group of Hispanics who further share a unique historical experience different from other Hispanics such as Puerto Ricans, Columbians, etc. Putting it in a different framework, Catholics are Christian and so are Baptists. Yet they differ in some beliefs.

(6) The Hispanic population is expected to become the largest minority group in the United States by the turn of the century. Mexican Americans are concentrated in the Southwest, the Farwest, and the Midwest.

(7) Schumann, p. 33.

(8) Schumann, John H., p. 64.

(9) The concept of cultural schizophrenia was advanced by Mark Clark in 1972 and is summarized by Brown, pp. 133-34. In such a situation the student views each encounter in the new culture as highly threatening and reacts in a very defensive manner.

(10) For an excellent overview of the Land Grants Issue see Rodolfo Acuna, *Occupied America* (San Francisco: The Canfield Press, 1972), pp. 43-45, 60-63, 67-69, 73-75 and 105, 106. Also, Carey McWilliams, *North From Mexico*, (New York: Greenwood Press, Publishers, 1968), p. 110 and Stan Steiner, *La Raza*, (New York: Harper and Row, Publishers, 1969), pp. 28-30, and 57-64.

(11) Culture shock is a disorientation which occurs when a person enters a new environment and finds that the problem-solving tools (e.g. language, values, points of reference, etc.) are inadequate for resolving his or her immediate needs. In the context of higher education the needs may include reading college level tests, writing essays, learning to "scout" teachers in advance, knowing how to take notes, being open with counselors or teachers concerning academic difficulties, etc., etc. Culture shock is supposedly a temporary phase in the mechanics of acculturation, the process whereby a person exchanges his or her first language and first culture for another language/culture. However, for the student who wishes to retain the first language/culture *and* also learn and equally function in a second language/culture, the culture shock experience may be quite lengthy. It would further appear that the ability or necessity to revert back to the environment of the first culture/language further lengthens the culture shock phase. For reservation-bound American Indians, barrio-rooted Hispanic and ghetto-resident black students, this reverting promotes the achievement of true bilingualism/biculturalism while simultaneously prolonging culture shock. For a further discussion on culture shock see Brown, pp. 131-135 and Schumann, pp. 31, 32.

# BIBLIOGRAPHY

Acuna, Rodolfo. *Occupied America: The Chicano's Struggle Toward Liberation.* San Francisco: Canfield Press, A Department of Harper & Row, Publishers, Inc., 1972.

Brown, H. Douglas. *Principles of Language Learning and Teaching.* Englewood Cliffs: Prentice-Hall, Inc., 1980.

King, Reatha Clark. "The Changing Student, A Resource for Improvement of Educational Services." *National Forum LXV,* 3 (Summer 1985): 22-27.

McWilliams, Carey. *North from Mexico.* Philadelphia: J.B. Lippincott Company, 1948; reprint ed., New York: Greenwood Press, Publishers, 1968.

Schumann, John H. "The Acculturation Model for Second Language Acquisition." In *Second-Language Acquisition & Foreign Language Teaching,* pp. 27-50. Edited by Rosario C. Gingas. Washington, D.C.: Center for Applied Linguistics, 1978.

Steiner, Stan. La Raza, *The Mexican Americans.* New York: Harper & Row, Publishers, 1969.

Stoner, Candy. "Minority Progress Under The Microscope." *School Product News,* July 1985, pp. 31-34.

# SUGGESTED ADDITIONAL READINGS

Birmingham, Stephen. *"The Rest of Us" The Rise of America's Eastern European Jews.* Boston: Little, Brown and Company, 1984.

Boswell, Thomas D. and Curtis, James R., *The Cuban-American Experience Culture, Images, and Perspectives.* Totowa: Rowman & Allanheld Publishers (A division of Littlefield, Adams, & Co.), 1983.

Duran, Livie Isauro, and Bernard, Russel H., eds., *Introduction to Chicano Studies, A Reader.* New York: Macmillan Publishing Co., Inc., 1973.

Fitzpatrick, Joseph P. *Puerto Rican Americans, The Meaning of Migration to the Mainland.* Prentice-Hall Ethnic Groups in American Life Series. Englewood Cliffs: Prentice-Hall, Inc., 1971.

Hall, William S., and Freedle, Roy O., *Culture and Language, The Black American Experience.* Washington: Hemisphere Publishing Corporation, 1975.

Laffin, John. *The Arab Mind Considered, A Need for Understanding.* New York: Taplinger Publishing Company, 1975.

Melendy, Brett H. *The Oriental Americans*. New York: Twayne Publishers, Inc., 1972.

Mendes-Flohr, Paul R. and Reinharz, Jehuda, eds. *The Jew in the Modern World, A Documentary History*. New York: Oxford University Press, 1980.

Montero, Daniel. *Vietnamese Americans: Patterns of Resettlement and Socio-Economic Adaption in the United States*. Forward by Chau Kim Nhan. Boulder, Co.: Westview Press, Inc., 1979.

Murdock, George Peter. *Outline of World Cultures*. New Haven: Human Relations Area Files, Inc., 1954. A very detailed index to world cultures updated in 1963 and available through interlibrary loan from a variety of libraries.

Nelson, Jack L., ed. *Values and Society*. Rochelle Park: Hayden Book Company, Inc., 1975.

Pinkney, Alphonso. *Black Americans*. Prentice-Hall Ethnic Groups in American Life Series. Englewood Cliffs: Prentice-Hall, Inc., 1969.

Richmond, Marie Laliberte. *Immigrant Population & Family Structure Among Cubans in Miami, Fl.* Hispanics in America Series. NY: Arno Press, A New York Times Company, 1980. Edited by Carlos E. Cortes.

Scasz, Margaret. *Education and the American Indian, The Road to Self-Determination, 1928-1973*. Albuquerque: University of New Mexico Press, 1974.

Stoddard, Ellwyn R. *Mexican Americans*. New York: Random House, Inc., 1973.

# Access, Excellence and Student Retention: A Leadership Commitment

Nolen M. Ellison
Janet D. Smith
Robert L. Green

## THE EXTENT AND NATURE OF STUDENT RETENTION AND DROPOUT

Meeting the special needs of high risk students in American higher education is a challenge for institutions as well as the broader society. The promise of open admissions has too often turned into a "revolving door" particularly at those institutions seeking to increase their enrollments by marketing their services to students who have traditionally not participated, or been excluded from higher education. While the challenges of access, standards, retention and graduation are equally compelling to two and four-year

Dr. Nolen M. Ellison is President of Cuyahoga Community College.
Dr. Janet D. Smith is the College's Associate Vice President for Planning and Research, Cuyahoga Community College.
Dr. Robert L. Green is the Coordinator of Cuyahoga Community College's Joint Center for Applied Research and Urban Education.

institutions of higher learning, it is the two year, low-cost, open access community and junior colleges which face the most significant challenge. It is these institutions which give meaning to a philosophy, and implement strategies which demonstrate that all persons *can* indeed, learn.

Nationwide, the problem of school leaving or dropout has assumed significant proportions at all levels of the educational system. The Education Commission of the States estimated in 1985 that each year 700,000, or one quarter of all American students at the high school level, drop out before graduating. This figure approaches approximately 50% for inner city schools (Institute for Educational Leadership, 1986). Numerous studies support these estimates and provide additional detail concerning the problem (General Accounting Office, 1986; Hodgkinson, 1986; Quinones, 1986a).

Statistical information on the number of students who drop out at the college level is far more difficult to acquire. Noel (1986) estimates that close to 30 percent of all persons entering college in any given year will not attend for their sophomore year. He estimates the figure to be at about the 46 percent level in public community colleges.

## Some Causes of Schooling Discontinuation

Many recent studies have attempted to understand why such inordinately large numbers of persons entering American colleges and universities fail to stay in school or to complete the requirements for graduation. The reasons for such failure frequently identified include financial difficulties (Lyke, 1985; Marinnaccio, 1985; Martin, 1986); family and personal problems or responsibilities (Institute for Educational Leadership, 1986; Sprandel, 1986); mental and physical problems (Quinones, 1986a) and poor academic preparation (Moore and Carpenter, 1986; Tinto, 1986). Some studies also take note of the low level of expectations and motivation evident in American youth at this point in the nation's history (Green, 1985; Marinaccio, 1985).

## The Cost of School Dropout

When a young person capable of earning a two or four-year college degree enrolls in an appropriate institution but fails to achieve stated educational goals, both the individual and the society sustain enormous financial losses. Henry Levin of Stanford University has estimated that $77 billion dollars are lost annually by society, mostly in the form of taxes on unrealized earnings, as a result of youth dropping out of high school (Institute for Educational Leadership, 1986). The loss of needed technical and other skills to the country at a time of greatly increased foreign competition compounds the costs which result from permanent discontinuation from formal schooling.

Financial and other losses to individual dropouts and to their families, including future spouses and children, are also staggering. Study after study documents the reduced earning power (Howell and Frese, 1982; General Accounting Office, 1986; Institute for Educational Leadership, 1986), the poorer physical and mental health, and the decreased opportunities in life (Howell and Frese, 1982; Institute for Educational Leadership, 1986) of dropouts. For a youth, who could do so, not to join that group of persons with two- or four-year college degrees is a significant personal as well as family loss. As the National Association for the Advancement of Colored People (NAACP) so aptly describes it, "a mind is a terrible think to waste."

## The Paradox of Access and Student Retention in Higher Education

Access to schooling at any level is a prior condition which must be understood and addressed before the important issue of student retention can be appropriately considered. Until the relatively recent past, trends across the country had not been to increase the degree of access to opportunities for college education for all who held such aspirations (Green, 1985). The phenomenal pattern of growth in student enrollments at community colleges since the early 1960s does, however, attest to the recognition that access to post-secondary education should be granted to everyone. Thus, increased access to American higher education, made possible in large part through these low tuition, "open door" community colleges, has now become a permanent expectation for all colleges and universities.

Community Colleges have always provided access to higher education for a wide range of "non-traditional" students with few or even no other educational options. With minimal restrictions to enrollment, such schools make available sound opportunities for an increasingly large pool of young people and adults who seek to complete two-year career or technical training or to pursue a two year course of study leading to an applied science degree. Community Colleges also provide opportunities for young people and adults who wish to prepare to move on to four-year baccalaureate degree-granting institutions. Disproportionate numbers of minority, financially disadvantaged and educationally underprepared students have therefore gravitated to two-year colleges (Olivas, 1979).

With fewer restrictive admission policies, community colleges are, however, generally more at risk than are four-year schools as regards the number of students who can be called dropouts. Community colleges are considerably more likely to accept students who would be rejected as "poor academic risks" by four-year colleges and universities. Thus, a relatively larger proportion of community college students tend to be less academically well-prepared than students enrolled in more traditional four-year schools.

Another factor pertinent to the student retention and dropout levels at community colleges is that a relatively high proportion of students work part-time or full-time while attending classes in order to obtain a two-year degree. Many such students have limited financial resources, and are at a greater risk of experiencing financial difficulties than is the case among students who enroll in four-year colleges and universities.

# SOME ISSUES RELATED TO STUDENT RETENTION AND DROPOUT

## Defining Student Retention and Dropout

A major failure of the statistics which describe present institutional efforts to retain students until they achieve their career goals relates to inadequate definitions and well-understood information concerning student retention and educational dropout. Incomplete definitions of these two terms hamper the accuracy of their measurements. They also restrict the nature and range of approaches to improving the opportunities for students to achieve their educational goals.

Admittedly, the reasons for school dropout usually cited in the literature do not altogether consider an appropriate distinction between students who frequently fail to participate in some predictable fashion in an educational program and those whose discontinued participation is temporary, but unpredictable, even though intended. This distinction is particularly relevant in estimating the statistics which describe the dropout rate among community and junior college students. The typical profile found in such populations is one of a twenty-six year old female head of household attending part-time and with responsibility for one or more children under the age of six. Such a student profile results in the completion of these traditional two-year degree programs only over a period of five to six years. The time to completion of traditional four-year degree programs are also affected by the changing student demographics. Two-year post-secondary educational institutions will continue to attract an increasingly more mature student population when compared to their four-year counterparts. The impact of family and employment responsibilities on a pattern of "intermittent" college attendance becomes an important consideration in defining student achievement of educational and career goals. Such goals frequently fall short of actual degree attainment.

To successfully consider the complex issue of student retention, particularly in higher education, it is, therefore, essential that more accurate working definitions be formulated. The following definitions are offered:

* Retention — The continued participation of students, intending to achieve some specific educational goal, in an educational system until such educational goals have been achieved or graduation occurs.

* Dropout — A student who formerly participated in a formal educational program with the intent of achieving some specific educational goal or of graduating but who terminated his or her affiliation with that or another degree-granting institution even though his or her circumstances were such that the student could have remained and "graduated" (Institute for Educational Leadership, 1986; Tinto, 1986).

* Intermittent Student — A student who has chosen to achieve his or her educational goal by moving alternately among job related career pursuits, formal educational experiences and personal leisure. It is difficult to classify this student in traditional higher education terms. An increasingly large proportion of today's two-year college students fall in this category.

The use of these definitions results in certain significant distinctions among college-going students. While degree-seeking students are still being considered, a less global distinction is suggested for "dropouts." A student is not a "dropout" if he or she transfers to another institution. More must also be understood about the "intermittent student" in order to assess where this student fits in decisions related to educational programming. An adult student who acquires the base knowledge and skills to move from a degree focused program into a career-work situation need also not be tallied as a college "dropout."

In considering these definitional issues, other practical matters related to student dropout emerge. Should a community college, for example, commit sizable amounts of its resources in order to "retain" students who wish to complete degree requirements on a continuing attendance basis as contrasted with others lacking the interest, preparation or personal circumstances which enable them to succeed in a less predictable fashion? Issues of mission as well as legal and moral questions come to mind. Such issues must, however, continue to be addressed if student retention efforts are to be systematically developed and sustained throughout all levels of education.

## The Importance of Student Retention Information

An educational institution committed to maximizing student retention cannot organize and operate an effective program without pertinent information (Morrow, 1986; Noel, 1986; Quinones, 1986a). Having no accurate data or figures on students who have dropped out or who are at risk to do so poses a serious disadvantage to effective program development. Just as important is the reliable knowledge concerning which institutional efforts have a positive impact on student retention. What kind of information would be useful in assessing student retention? Such information may be either student or program-centered (Levitz, 1986). Systematic collection and utilization of both program and student data for evaluation and program improvement purposes must be an integral part of any strategy related to the degree completion of to other educational goal attainment of students.

*Student-Centered Information.* Educational institutions invariably collect certain information on students on a periodic basis. They are thus in a position to conduct some limited analyses of students who graduate or who fail to do so. Careful analysis of additional student-centered information related to retention policies and practices would greatly reduce the amount of guesswork which enters the process of developing and maintaining effective student retention programs. Yet, how many institutions have identified the pertinent student data to collect on retention policies, have obtained and updated it, have analyzed it, and have then established and operated programs based on such data driven knowledge and expectations? The literature suggests that the number is indeed few (Astin, 1975; Mann, 1985; Levitz and Noel, 1986; Morrow, 1986).

Institutional policy makers and program management staffs will be better positioned to do strategic as well as operational planning with access to pertinent information that is properly analyzed. Strong institutional commitment to student access, retention and graduation will be required to provide justification for research and evaluation strategies which call for maintenance of such information and data analyses in order to enhance planning, however. Answers to what kinds of questions are critical to effective student retention programs? For example, what factors correlate with students' stay in college? Which students are the most likely candidates for non-educational goal attainment? Properly focused information which addresses these and other useful policy issues ranges from program based cost-benefit analyses to student learning outcomes. Institutions working alone or with such organizations as The College Entrance Examination Board (CEEB) and Educational Testing Service (ETS) are well-advised to make such information available as an integral part of their planning for improvements in student retention.

*Program-Centered Information.* Effective student retention programming also requires the use of information concerning academic and non-academic programs, including those not necessarily perceived as directly related to student retention (Kramer *et al.,* 1985; Marinaccio, 1985; Smith, Lippett and Sprandel, 1986). Academic and student services intervention strategies, properly linked with student support initiatives, can affect student dropout rates. For example, colleges which do not offer basic remedial courses, yet admit large numbers of students who are not adequately prepared academically will not be able to retain large proportions of their students. This student loss will be caused, in part, by the academic program and staff that is available (Noel and Levitz, 1983; Kramer *et al.,* 1985; Moore and Carpenter, 1986). Schools with instructional staff who teach at sub-standard levels may also expect to see the more ambitious students "dropping out" if other options are available. Thus, it is important that educational institutions create stronger "matches" between their academic programs and the student body they serve. Reliable and pertinent information on students as well as on aspects of the academic and student services program are therefore crucial to making decisions concerning these areas.

## THE NEED FOR COMPREHENSIVE STUDENT RETENTION PROGRAMS

The dilemma of student retention has always plagued educational institutions. The extent of such dilemma has varied with the location of institutions and the economic and other demographic characteristics of their students. Only in recent years have thoughtful, well-organized efforts been undertaken, however, to understand the significant attributes of effective student retention programs. It is even more recently that focused attention has been given to establishing and operating programs designed to reduce the numbers of students who would otherwise fail to complete their short or long-term educational goals. (Kramer *et al.*, 1985; Lyke, 1985; Noel, 1986; Quinones, 1986.) Growing public awareness of the crisis has helped to encourage student retention efforts (Institute for Educational Leadership, 1986). The increasing inability of higher education institutions to retain the changing (demography) of students to the completion of their educational goals has also been an important incentive for focused program development efforts.

The nature of the crisis, the grown knowledge, and increased appreciation of the costs of discontinued education to society and to individuals make it imperative that effective, coordinated retention programs become an essential feature of educational institutions. Indeed, it may be argued that anything less than a total commitment to student retention speaks well for educational failure. Such failure on the part of the nation's educational community and its supporters will result only in larger numbers of young people and adults who are unable to function effectively in their own as well, it will impact on the economic and social development of their families, communities and of themselves.

Though virtually every modern educational institution directs some of its effort toward student retention, many such efforts are, at best, fragmented (Institute for Educational Leadership, 1986; Morrow, 1986). They typically operate with a dearth of pertinent information (Astin, 1975; Levitz, 1986), are understaffed (Kramer, 1985; Marinaccio, 1985), and are seldom based on clearly formulated, understood or attainable goals and objectives (Noel, 1986). Many higher education institutions have utilized Title III (Developing Institutions), Tri-O (Access) and other special federal and state programs to organize, structure and implement their student recruitment and retention programs. However, because the causes which under lie and are associated with increasing rates of student dropout and patterns of intermittent educational participation are complex in nature, programs which are not comprehensive and well designed tend to be inadequate or ineffective (Astin, 1975; Marinaccio, 1986; Smith, Lippitt and Sprandel, 1986).

*Individual Assessment Programs:* Increased attention to student testing and assessment programs aimed at facilitating their placement in the most appropriate courses is also important to designed programs which give the best assurance of student success, hence retention. Project Equality (EQ) sponsored by the College Board and other special programs available through the Educational Testing Services (ETS), which focus on the need for student assessment are examples of available resources which can be useful in structuring programs to improve student retention and graduation rates, both at the high school and college levels.

# ORGANIZING AND OPERATING A COMPREHENSIVE RETENTION PROGRAM: A LEADERSHIP COMMITMENT

It may be assumed that no conventional educational institution completely lacks some effort aimed at improving the retention of its students. Accordingly, it must be recognized that new retention programs are not established without some history and structural context. Designing and implementing comprehensive effective retention programs must therefore take into account existing programs and activities (Noel, 1986).

Given the non-original nature of such programs, what is required on the part of institutional leadership is a clear commitment to strategy planning and model building that does not "reinvent the wheel." Clear definition of existing roles and responsibilities of staff should be reviewed carefully prior to adding new staff to address access, retention and special needs programming. Strategic planning techniques can be useful in redefining, restructuring and implementing comprehensive retention programs that have a high probability of improving institutional performance in this important area. Special counseling, student service and academic support programs, funded through outside grants, should be integrated into a preplanned institutional strategy and design if maximum success is to be achieved. Vestibule, or special programs that are organized and operated on the periphery, with little connection to the core programs of the institution, do little to enhance the long term success of retention and graduation programs designed for special populations. The primary objective of such "special" initiatives must be their catalytic value in creating change in the basic core of the institution.

## Designing an Organizational Structure for Student Retention

A "generic" organizational chart for a comprehensive program model of the kind described in this chapter would include the elements shown in Figure 1. The executive officer responsible for the planning, development and implementation of a comprehensive student retention program would be accountable directly to the President of the institution. The high level of support, visibility and the sensitivity to policy formulation at the highest level of the institution, that is inherent in a total commitment to student retention requires such an approach (Kramer et al., 1985; Quinones, 1986a).

# ORGANIZATIONAL STRUCTURE
## COMPREHENSIVE STUDENT RETENTION PROGRAM MODEL

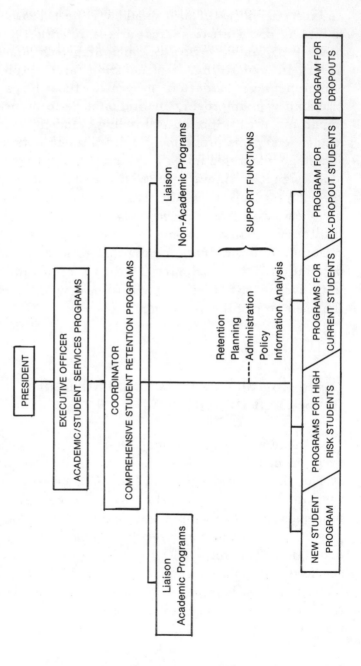

An important strength of the program would be those components specifically designed to coordinate pertinent academic and non-academic activities and programs which are deemed to significantly affect student retention. In such a model, jurisdictional issues would have to be dealt with. Clearly stated policies as well as effective use of interpersonal skills and informal management practices applicable to comprehensive student retention program (CSRP) coordination will help resolve questions of this nature.

Internal to the program would be a number of mainstay components — primarily those related to academic and non-academic program coordination and feedback. Additional components designed to work directly with various identified segments of the student body — students at risk; new students; current dropouts; and former dropouts who have returned would also be essential. A discussion of dropout prevention strategies focusing on the latter student groups, for the purpose of building and implementing such a model, appears later in this chapter.

An effective student retention program will also be concerned with the development and implementation of internal policies and procedures; the formulation of feasible goals and objectives and the ongoing evaluation of the processes as well as outcomes of student retention efforts. The operation of the program would be planned as an integral part of plans developed for the academic year. Specialized information-gathering activities and efforts focusing on encouraging students to return to the institution, however, would take place throughout the year. These latter efforts would also demonstrate to the community and the student body the institution's commitment to retention through any practical means.

## Elements of a Comprehensive
## Student Retention Program

Comprehensive retention programs should be designed to include the following elements and operations:

* A centrally planned and managed, comprehensive student retention program offices charged with responsibility for operating and/or coordinating the institution's activities relating to retention and dropout issues (Marinaccio, 1985; Noel, 1986; Quinones, 1986a). A direct commitment from the institutional leader with clear delegation of responsibility to a major line officer, normally the Vice President or Dean of Student or Academic Services, is essential to the successful development and implementation of this student retention model.

* The incorporation, with needed modifications of all pre-existing retention programs and program components, from student services and academic affairs, into the comprehensive student retention program as appropriate (Noel, 1986).

* An ongoing mechanism for data collection, analysis and reporting related to academic programs and offerings and non-academic programs and activities in order to identify the positive as well as negative effects of such programs and services in encouraging students to complete their education and career goals (Noel, 1986).

* The establishment and operation of the comprehensive student retention program within the context of clearly defined goals, objectives and expected outcomes. These should be developed in conjunction with the design of pertinent evaluation methodologies to be applied to the program.

## Some Dropout Prevention Strategies

The primary goal of a comprehensive student retention program is to maximize the number of students who graduate from, or otherwise achieve their education and career goals by attending the institution. Every student who leaves the institution, having accomplished a clearly defined set of goals, should be considered a "victory" for the comprehensive student retention program. Many student retention strategies have been tested over many years in a variety of academic settings (Astin, 1975; Lyke, 1985; Ellison, 1986; Institute for Educational Leadership, 1986; Noel, 1986). Among the more common dropout prevention strategies defined in terms of program components are orientation programs for new students, financial assistance programs, programs promoting a sense of community and academic excellence, as well as other direct personal assistance supports.

*New Students' Orientation.* One of the most common activities which academic institutions undertake to encourage students to remain in school is to demonstrate a welcoming, caring, respectful environment through a well planned new student orientation program. Such programs encourage and offer opportunities for new students to participate in the student community at the earliest possible time. They also communicate to them the institution's concern and interest in their well-being and adjustment to the new setting.

Schools which lack sound freshman orientation and advising programs and which make little effort to help new students become a part of the educational community do themselves a disservice as regards retention. Providing information on the goals, activities, and accomplishments of such programs to students is also of importance to a well coordinated retention program (Kramer *et al.,* 1985; Smith, Lippitt and Sprandel, 1986; Titley, 1986).

*Financial Assistance Programs.* Many students choose to discontinue pursuit of their educational goals because of financial considerations. Comprehensive student retention program activities must be designed to assist in maximizing the amount and kinds of funds available to students (Martin, 1986). Such assistance may take the form of loans, work opportunities or assistance in job placement in the community.

Scholarships and the availability of a wide range of other financial assistance programs play a central role in helping institutions to retain students. This is especially true when large numbers of economically "disadvantaged" young people and adults with limited income to support both education and family comprise the majority of the student body. Institutions sensitive to such student needs will endeavor to make a wide range of financial supports available. They will also make the best continuing use of the information available on the relationships between student retention and various forms of financial assistance (Lyke, 1985; Martin, 1986). In the latter regard, efforts to link co-operative education and work study programs to the career objectives and academic goals of students as part of a strategy for linking aspirations and hopes with meaningful life experiences are also useful financial support considerations.

*Programs Promoting a Sense of Community.* Persons who feel they are a part of, or members of, a special community are less likely to leave that community of shared goals and experiences, in numerous ways, that this can be an important asset in student retention. That educational institutions typically promote a sense of community, of shared goals and experiences, in numerous ways. An active student government respected by the institution; clearly defined mechanisms for two-way communication among administrators, faculty and students; the availability of a wide range of support systems and support groups; and the active involvement of the institution in its own larger community are all areas which help to develop a feeling of community membership among students.

*Programs Promoting Academic Excellence.* Efforts to maintain an atmosphere that is conducive to learning are also required in order to increase student retention. It is therefore important that institutions assess themselves against well known criteria for effective schooling (Green, 1985). These principles and criteria have been proven particularly appropriate in a number of school districts, such as Detroit, Memphis, Philadelphia and Cleveland. A pilot test of the applicability of this essential model is currently being tested at Cuyahoga Community College's Metropolitan Campus. The criteria for effective schooling include effective instructional leadership, a safe and orderly environment, systematic assessment and feedback concerning student progress, a climate of high expectations and a focus on effective student preparation in basic skills.

*Other Direct Assistance Programs.* Other non-academic services which offer help to students who wish to remain in school vary with students needs. They include career counseling (Lyke, 1985; Sprandel, 1986); health counseling (including programs on substance abuse prevention and treatment) (Kramer *et al.*, 1985; Quinones, 1986); and family, job and psychological counseling. For many students, the presence of religious supports and services may also be an important factor in their continued persistence to complete career and educational goals. Housing assistance and help in dealing with governmental institutions and processes are also important. An effective comprehensive student retention program will include program referral services which focus on these and similar areas of student needs. The coordination of the efforts of the comprehensive student retention program with those of other non-academic and community programs and groups must also be developed and nurtured.

The collection and use of processes and outcomes of programs is of critical importance in assessing institutional efforts to retain students. The dissemination of information to current, as well as potential students concerning the availability and confidentiality of these services is also important. Institutions with a wide range of assistance programs which do not make this information available, or which make the process of obtaining such assistance unduly difficult, delimit their ability both to attract and to retain students.

## Retention of Special Student Groups

A comprehensive student retention program, it is clear, will include carefully designed components related to planning, policy formulation, evaluation and other support functions of effective programs. Such a program will also require specialized activities designed to meet the needs of at least three special categories of students. These three groups are as follows:

* Students who may reasonably be expected (e.g., because of pre-college preparation) to be at greater risk of educational discontinuation than their fellow students.
* Students who have interrupted their schooling, but who may reasonably be expected to re-enroll at some time in the future; and
* Students who have previously interrupted their schooling, but who have returned to continue toward some education or career goal.

A student retention program which focuses only on the special needs of these three categories of students would generally not be appropriate for the majority of students for whom prevention is the most important goal. The needs of these three categories of students, along with intervention strategies appropriate to them, are described below.

*Students at Risk.* A review of research findings and careful reflections on one's experience with students should quickly make it clear that students possessing certain attributes are more prone to pose a challenge to their retention than are students without these attributes (General Accounting Office, 1986; Kilstad and Owings, 1986; Quinones, 1986a). Students "at risk" to discontinue their education are found most often in one or more of the following groups:

* Freshmen and other new students (Titley, 1986).
* Students with poor academic preparation (Moore and Carpenter, 1986).
* Students with a history of having dropped out of other educational institutions (Tinto, 1986).
* Students who are experiencing, or who may be expected to experience, financial difficulties (Martin, 1986).

Early identification based on analysis of information (grades, attendance, financial status, health status, etc.) to identify students who are at risk, followed by clearly defined strategies for intervention in accordance with established policies and practices coordinated by a "case manager" assigned to an individual student, would constitute the framework for early intervention to avoid academic failure and dropout.

*Former Students.* Carefully targeted activities would also focus on students who have already "dropped out" in order to determine the reason for such actions. Intervention would have the goal of encouraging and assisting them in returning to continue their education (Tinto, 1986). It should be recalled, however, that students manifest their "dropout" status from education in a variety of ways. One student may stop attending classes, another may "announce" in the middle of a semester that he or she will not return for the ensuring term. Yet another may call attention to a need for assistance by a visible lack of interest or motivation while attending classes on a regular basis. Opportunities to intervene with students who are likely to drop out will range from many to none.

When the opportunity offers itself, and even if the dropout action appears inevitable, an exit interview between the student and appropriate comprehensive student retention program staff is strongly recommended (Marinaccio, 1985). Well designed survey instruments, modified through time to benefit from experience with particular categories of students, should be used to elicit pertinent information concerning the reasons for leaving. Over time, the analysis of stated or assumed reasons for students' departures prior to achievement of educational goals would help to determine whether the institution should expend the resources required to re-enroll former dropouts in the institution. For the latter purpose, students leaving the institution would be categorized in terms of only two groups: Those remaining in the local area who have not enrolled in another academic institution, and whose circumstances are such that they could, in the near or later future, continue their education, and all other non-returning students, on the other hand.

Activities to encourage and assist dropouts to re-enroll would then only be directed at former students who meet the criteria in the first category (Pappas and Loring, 1986).

Prescribed retention or re-enrollment activities designed for specific students would address the reason(s) why each student dropped out. For example, financial problems would be dealt with by an expert in financial aid matters; family problems would be dealt with through appropriate counseling services internal to the institution or located within the community. In all cases, a designated "case manager" would serve as a facilitator and advocate for the student, securing and otherwise providing needed services.

*Returning Students.* A variety of circumstances may be encountered among students who dropped out but have returned to the institution to work toward completion of their education. At one end of a continuum, such a student may have dropped out for one term for health or other personal reasons but always intended to return. At the other end of the continuum may be a marginal student in need of extensive academic preparation, financial support and personal or other counseling who was "talked into trying another term" by his or her counselor, family or fellow students. A detailed assessment is therefore recommended for each student returning after a minimal period of absence. The purpose of this assessment of skills, goals and needs would aid in the development of an individualized plan of activities and services to maximize the chances of achieving defined goals (Pappas and Loring, 1986).

## Evaluating Student Retention Programs

Sound, useful evaluation of retention program requires the selection and design of pertinent and realistic program goals and objectives as well as intervention strategies and processes. It also presumes that clear statements of expected outcomes, accountabilities and data collection methods be formulated as an integral part of the program design and development phase, rather than after the program has become operational (Suchman, 1967). It is also important that pertinent information be collected before a program begins its operation and thus, before changes in modifiable behaviors and other indicators of success can be affected.

Because the development of comprehensive student retention programs will almost invariably take place in a context of previously existing programs and services, it will not be feasible in most cases to establish the most desirable evaluation component under ideal circumstances. Recognition of these ideals should, however, guide the preparation of a design that is both practical and useful.

The primary purpose of the evaluation should be to guide program adjustment, resource allocation and program planning. Applied research and evaluation findings will allow a college or university President or The Director of a comprehensive retention program to distinguish, with a relative degree of assurance, program components which "work" and others which do not. Such information will also determine the degree to which practices are useful in improving student retention and academic performance. The objectivity (often best stated in numerical terms) of outcome data is also important. Short- and long-term trend lines which describe program impact can, for example, be established and charted. The appropriate design and implementation of an effective evaluation scheme will compel periodic review of actual progress toward expected outcomes for program goals and objectives, stated in ways that are measurable (Suchman, 1967; Quinones, 1986a). This would be the case for both process and outcome goals.

While an effective student retention program would have its ongoing evaluation performed by qualified persons not directly associated with the program, it is important that staff be directly involved in understanding the design and results of analyses; that they clearly understand the nature of expected outcomes and the measures which most appropriately reflect such outcomes. Program performance against stated goals and objectives would occur at least annually, and would be undertaken with the practical application of the findings always in mind. In the latter regard, it would be expected that program components and practices that are found to be effective, and for which the need in fact exists, would be firmly institutionalized. Components and practices determined to be less effective or even counterproductive to student retention would be appropriately modified or eliminated throughout the institution.

That student retention program goals and objectives are stated in clearly defined terms for objective verification and measurement cannot be overstated. Examples of primary and secondary goals which might be appropriate for a comprehensive retention program include such statements as the following:

* To reduce the number of dropouts, as defined, from 37

percent of the total student body (as calculated for the 86-87
school year) to 35 percent, 33 percent and 31 percent
respectively for the 1987-1988, 1988-1989, and 1989-1990
school years.

* To accomplish the major goals of the program, as stated, on
  budgets of $X,000, $Y,000, $Z,000 respectively for the 1987-
  1988, 1988-1989, and 1989-1990 school years.

* To enhance the freshman orientation program such that
  during their first full month of enrollment, students will
  have completed a weekend program consisting of 12 hours
  of programming, and three evening events of three hours
  each — the 18 hours to be devoted to introducing them to the
  school and the school community, and to consist of
  information concerning (specified) topics.

These brief examples indicate the degree to which careful
preparation and statement of goals and objectives will greatly
facilitate the evaluation process and the applicability of the
findings to mid course changes related to such areas as
planning, scheduling, control, coordination and supervision of
program activities as well as resource allocation.

# STUDENT RETENTION AT CUYAHOGA COMMUNITY COLLEGE — A CASE STUDY

For over two decades, Cuyahoga Community College has
responded to the dilemma of educational access and
opportunity for urban and minority students. The efforts of the
College have resulted in measurable success, but the
institution also acknowledges that much of the challenge still
remains to be met.

In attempting to help students overcome both personal and
structural barriers to higher education, Cuyahoga Community
College has focused primarily on a strategy of inter-
institutional articulation. This strategy seeks to smooth the

transitions students must make from secondary schools to two-year schools to four-year schools and to improve the chances of their retention at each of these levels. The major elements of change affected by Cuyahoga Community College's articulation approach are curricular improvements, academic and student support services, development of student information systems and enhancement of transfer agreements and opportunities.

As it began its third decade, Cuyahoga Community College established a five year strategy (1984-1989) to improve educational access, opportunity, retention and success for students seeking associate and baccalaureate degrees. Each element of this effort was designed to operate within the context of Cuyahoga Community College's overall strategic planning and institutional development framework.

Thus, on October 1, 1984, the College established a Center for Articulation and Transfer Opportunities (CATO). The Center's mandates were to provide institution-wide leadership, coordination, evaluation, policy research and reporting services, particularly as they relate to enhancement of articulation, retention and transfer opportunities.

During 1986, Cuyahoga Community College further recognized a need to take full advantage of its rapidly growing programs and resources related to improving the access and retention in educational programs of young people before and during post-secondary education. What was needed was a more effective theoretical framework that would provide a "map" for the College's longitudinal strategy for institutional change. The College's Urban Demonstration Model addresses that need. It describes a theoretical context for the College's coordinated efforts to facilitate high school to college transitions; improve student retention and academic achievement; and facilitate two-year to four-year college transfer. Cuyahoga Community College's Urban Demonstration Model also provides an institutional framework for evaluations and analyses designed to assess the accomplishment of goals for both program outcomes and institutional change.

The Urban Demonstration Model was developed as a collaborative and aggressive strategy for effective schooling in a large urban area. It addresses the College's acknowledgment that, to ensure the success of large groups of minority students in two-year colleges, an institution must develop a strategy that is clearly tied to a collegewide sense of purpose and priority. The model delineates a set of theoretical principles, the expected outcomes, institutional structure and operational responsibilities involved in such an undertaking.

The decision to launch a full-fledged and highly coordinated model to enhance minority student access, retention and success is grounded in some fundamental premises. These are summarized below:

* Consistent with its mission and philosophy, an institution must undertake change to improve minority student success in a way that is clearly understood and reflected as a *strategy for overall institutional advancement.*
* Effective strategy requires that *cooperative relationships* be developed with urban high schools and four-year colleges and universities in the interest of students who will enter and exit at these levels of the educational continuum.
* A *clear definition and well-understood theoretical framework* (including expected outcomes and evaluation measures) must govern the development of efforts to effect both short and long term institutional change.
* Executive leadership is an important key to institutional change. However, in the absence of singular line reporting relationships, *clearly defined structural relationships and accountability structures* are required.

Of particular significance to its student retention programming is the development of its theoretical framework for student success as a means of organizing and implementing programs designed to implement the Urban Demonstration Model.

The purpose of any theory or framework is to establish a sense of order around which objectives for accomplishing relevant outcomes can be developed. Because institutional change to improve student retention and success requires that coherence be created from seemingly disparate functions in structurally different areas, such a sense of order is particularly important. It provides the pegs on which to hang each activity and simultaneously describes the contribution of each objective. A theoretical framework also serves to define a set of institutional outcomes against which the implementation of plans can be evaluated. Decisions concerning program modification, resource allocation and the placement of institutional responsibilities are also facilitated.

In the case of Cuyahoga Community College, "effective schools" theory provides the beginning framework around which to organize programmatic efforts to increase opportunities and improve the likelihood of student retention and educational success, particularly among minority students. Through extensive faculty and administrative discussions, program review and analysis and thorough review of the effective schools' literature, this theoretical model is being modified and expanded to meet the needs of both high school and community college students. Much of the research, evaluation and writing on effective schools in the past has focused on student achievement at the elementary and middle school levels. Cuyahoga Community College is providing national leadership in the application of this theory at the high school and community college levels.

In addition to presenting academic credibility, this theory is also sufficiently inclusive and adaptable to accommodate the broad range of objectives which are required to improve institutional effectiveness. The factors which have been shown to distinguish effective from ineffective schools, and are adapted below as the theoretical framework for Cuyahoga Community College's Urban Demonstration Model are the following:

* A statement of *school mission* that is clearly defined, communicated to, and understood by its public as well as by its administrators, teachers and students.

* An emphasis on *school-community relations* (parents, businesses, civic organizations) that is required for cooperative planning implementation and support of educational programs. This exemplifies and communicates to students the mission and purpose of schools, the expectations of exemplary performance, the nature of teacher support that is available to assure such performance and the individual's responsibility for learning.

* An emphasis on *academic foundations* that is associated with students' ability to read, write, compute and process information with a minimum level of difficulty.

* A *school learning climate* that cultivates respect and mutually trusting relationships among students, teachers and administrators in a manner that enhances student learning.

* Strong and effective *leadership,* particularly in the instructional and student support domains. Such leadership confers with and advises teachers and students about learning outcomes and assures prompt solutions to enhance support for the school.

* *High expectations* are grounded on a belief that all students can achieve well beyond their current levels, and that student learning is a responsibility shared by both teachers and learners. Teachers are expected to provide high quality instruction, and to maintain high standards of learning. Students are expected to function at the highest motivational, perseverance and capability levels,

and to accept personal responsibility for their performance.
* Continuous *instructional assessment and feedback* that
  are used to motivate students as well as to form the basis of
  corrective action. The objectives of instruction, along with
  the level of skills, knowledge and competencies which
  students are expected to learn must be clearly understood
  by each student.

The theoretical principles described above will be assessed in terms of their applicability to instructional and support programs jointly or separately designed and administered by Cuyahoga Community College, other cooperating colleges and universities, and urban public high schools in Northeastern Ohio.

Current modifications to the Model for student retention established at Cuyahoga Community College is taking place to further assure that the institution remains responsive and responsible in its efforts to address the changing needs of its student body. The Urban Demonstration Model is, for example, now being structured to create articulation linkages with public schools on one end and colleges and universities on the other. These "bridges" across the three levels of education are designed to encourage students to continue toward their educational goals with the assurance of well integrated curricula ladders, educational plans, integrated personal, academic and career support systems (including financial aid planning) as well as monitoring, record keeping and feedback related to their progress (Ellison & Smith, 1986).

# CONCLUSION

Problems associated with high school and college dropout rates have reached a level such that a substantial response is called for from the academic community as well as others concerned with the future of America. Effective retention programs at the college and university level are, in general, in their infancy. They operate in a context lacking a generally accepted body of research and practices that have been deemed effective. That there is not yet a commonly agreed upon definition of the term "dropout" is ample evidence of issues related to the best approaches to address the dilemma of student retention.

The urgency of the problem, however, requires that attempts be made to design appropriate models of student retention programs, at least conceptually. It would appear appropriate, based on the findings to date, that a model retention program would be comprehensive; centralized; reporting directly to the executive officer with leadership responsibility for academic and student support services; and capable of extensive information gathering and analysis. Such a model would include program components differentiated for various student populations in addition to its "all student" approach and would be evaluated through a carefully designed formative evaluation process. Given the current state of the art in retention research and programs, it would likewise be appropriate that models of student retention programs maintain considerable room for flexibility in their design. Such flexibility would allow for needed changes, as determined by the results of on-going evaluation and student needs information.

## REFERENCES

Astin, A.W., *Preventing Students from Dropping Out*. San Francisco: Jossey-Bass, 1975.

Bielby, W.T., Models of Status Attainment in Treimen, D.J. and Robinson, R.V. (Eds.), *Researching Social Stratefication and Mobility Volume 1*, Greenwich: JAI Press, 1981.

Ellison, N.M. and Smith, J.D., "Access and Excellence: The Articulation Challenge Among Urban High Schools, Community College, and Four-Year Institutions," in *Toward Mastery Leadership in Access, Assessment, and Developmental Education*, John S. Keyser and Deborah L. Floyd, Editors. ACT, 1987.

Ellison, N.M., Smith J.D. and Green, R.L. "Mapping Aggressive Strategy for Improving the Success of Minority Students" unpublished paper, Office of Institutional Planning and Research, Cuyahoga Community College, 1986.

General Accounting Office, School Dropouts: The Extent and Nature of the Problem, GAO/HRD-86-106BR. A Briefing Report to Congressional Requesters, June, 1986.

Green, R.L. *The Urban Challenge: Poverty and Race.* Chicago: Follett Publishing Co., 1977.

Green, Robert L., "Student Access to Higher Education in Cities: Social Responsibility and Excellence," address delivered to the National Association of State Universities and Land-Grant Colleges, Tampa, FL. March, 1985.

Hodgkinson, H.L., All One System: Demographics of Education, Kindergarten Through Graduate School, Institute for Educational Leadership, June, 1985.

Howell, F.M. and Frese, W., *Making Life Plans: Race, Gender and Career Decisions,* Washington: University Press of America, 1982.

Institute for Educational Leadership, *School Dropouts: Everybody's Problem,* 1986.

Kramer, G.L. *et al.,* "Why Students Persist in College: A Categorical Analysis," *NACADA Journal,* 5 (2), October, 1985.

Kolstad, A.J. and Owings, J.A., *High School Dropouts Who Change Their Minds About School,* U.S. Department of Education, Office of Educational Research Improvement, April, 1986.

Levitz, R. and Noel, L., "Using a Systematic Approach to Assessing Retention Needs," in Noel, L.; Levitz, R.; and Saluri, D. (Eds.), *Increasing Student Retention.* San Francisco: Jossey-Bass, 1986.

Lyke, R. "A Short Summary of the Federal Dropout Prevention Program," Congressional Research Service, Library of Congress, May, 1985.

Mann, D. "Action of Dropouts," In *Educational Leadership,* 43 (1), September, 1985.

Marinaccio, J., "Attrition at Community Colleges in Current Issues for the Community College": Essays by Fellows in the Mid-Career Fellowship Program at Princeton University, September, 1985.

Martin, A.D., Jr. "Financial Aid," in Noel, L.; Levitz, R.; and Saluri, D. (Eds.), *Increasing Student Retention,* San Francisco: Jossey-Bass, 1986.

Moore, W., Jr. and Carpenter, L.N. "Academically Unprepared Students," in Noel, L.; Levitz, R.; and Saluri, D. (Eds.), *Increasing Student Retention,* San Francisco: Jossey-Bass, 1986.

Morrow, G., "Standardizing Practice in the Analysis of School Dropouts," *Teachers' College Record,* 87 (3), Spring, 1986.

Noel, L. and Levitz, R., *National Dropout Study,* American College Testing Program National Center for Advancement of Educational Practices, Iowa City, IA, 1983.

Noel, L., "Increasing Student Retention: New Challenges and Potential," in Noel, L.; Levitz, R.; and Saluri, D. (Eds.), *Increasing Student Retention,* San Francisco: Jossey-Bass, 1986.

Olivias, Michael J., *The Dilemma of Access: Minorities in Two-Year Colleges,* Howard University Press, Washington, D.C. 1979.

Pappas, J.P. and Loring, R.K., "Returning Learners," in Noel, L.; Levitz, R.; and Saluri, D. (Eds.), *Increasing Student Retention,* San Francisco: Jossey-Bass, 1986.

Quinones, N., *Dropout Prevention Programs:* 1985-1986, Progress Report, New York City Board of Education, Special Circular #25, May 21, 1986a.

Quinones, N., *Tentative Guidelines for 1986-1987 School-Based Dropout Prevention Programs in the New York City Public School System,* New York City Board of Education, Special Circular #25, May 21, 1986b.

Roueche, J.E. and Baker III, G.A., *Access and Excellence: The Open Door College,* The Community College Press, 1987.

Sprandel, H.Z., "Career Planning and Counseling," in Noel, L.; Levitz, R.; and Saluri, D. (Eds.), *Increasing Student Retention,* San Francisco: Jossey-Bass, 1986.

Suchman, E.A. *Evaluative Research.* New York; Russell Sage Foundation, 1967.

Smith, L.N.; Lippitt, R.; and Sprandel, D., "Building Support for the Campuswide Retention Program," in Noel, L.; Levitz, R.; and Saluri, D. (Eds.), *Increasing Student Retention,* San Francisco: Jossey-Bass, 1986.

Tinto, V., Dropping Out and Other "Forms of Withdrawal from College," in Noel, L.; Levitz, R.; and Saluri, D. (Eds.), *Increasing Student Retention,* San Francisco: Jossey-Bass, 1986.

Titley, B.S. "Orientation Programs," in Noel, L.; Levitz, R.; and Saluri, D. (Eds.), *Increasing Student Retention,* San Francisco: Jossey-Bass, 1986.

# A Conceptual Framework and Change Strategy for Improving Faculty Evaluation Programs

## Al Smith

*With many different approaches to faculty and staff evaluation in colleges and universities, how can a conceptual framework and change strategy be used to develop a new or revised staff evaluation program?*

Conceptual frameworks for faculty and staff evaluation existed in the world's earliest colleges and universities. The

**Al Smith** is a Professor of Educational Leadership and Assistant Director of the Institute of Higher Education at the University of Florida, Gainesville, and is Director of the National Faculty Evaluation Project for Colleges and Universities. He has addressed national conferences on the subjects of faculty evaluation and development and consulted widely in these two fields. He received his Ph.D. degree from the Center for the Study of Higher Education at the University of Michigan in 1970.

frameworks used then were somewhat different from the ones being considered in colleges today. In universities around the time of 1000 A.D. students often hired and dismissed faculty members, while faculty members employed the college administrative staff. These rather unique approaches have changed over the years. Today college boards of trustees and administrators have assumed much of the responsibility for developing staff evaluation policy and procedure. This shift in the focus of responsibility for evaluation has not lessened the need for effective programs. Nor has this shift in the conceptualization of the program lessened the need for the involvement of faculty or staff in the development of new policies and procedures.

The need for a clearer conception of the faculty/staff evaluation process has increased for a variety of reasons in recent years. Some of these reasons include: 1. stabilizing or declining enrollments, 2. increasingly tenured-in departments, meaning less mobile and aging college faculties, 3. declining financial resources, and 4. the realization that all staff members, not just the full-time faculty, are important to the successful achievement of a college's mission statements, goals, and program objectives. In institutions where as much as 60 to 90 percent of the budget goes toward the payment of faculty salaries, the need for a strong faculty evaluation and development program is evident. For these reasons and in order to achieve their many purposes, institutions of higher learning need a conceptual framework for faculty (both full and part-time) evaluation that will result in the maximum utilization of their human capital, their most vital resource.

A conceptual framework for any university, college, or department faculty evaluation program must begin with a description of the purposes for that system. Few college educational programs or staff evaluation programs will succeed without clearly defined and accepted purposes. Conceptually, then, what have been the major purposes for most faculty or staff evaluation programs? In a regional survey of faculty evaluation practices conducted by the Southern Regional Education Board (SREB), the investigators found that the various reasons for faculty evaluation could be reduced to essentially "1. a concern for faculty development and improvement and 2. the need for evaluation of faculty performance to provide information for decisions on tenure, promotion, reappointment, and salary" (Boyd and Schietinger, 1976, p. 1). These two reasons, development and evaluation, are the same reasons being given to justify most faculty evaluation schemes today. A third reason that is becoming quite popular is for the purpose of making merit pay decisions. All three of these purposes should be considered for incorporation into any new or revised staff evaluation scheme in the 1980s and 1990s. The relative extent to which any one of these purposes is stressed will in turn greatly influence the type of faculty evaluation program developed at any given college.

A variety of conceptual frameworks for achieving the purposes of faculty and staff evaluation have been proposed in recent years. In the remaining sections of this chapter, these conceptual frameworks will be reviewed briefly. In addition, the Southern Regional Education Board's "Framework for Developing the Components of a Systematic Faculty Evaluation Program" and a fourteen step, three year strategy for the development of successful faculty evaluation programs will be reviewed. Finally, the successful application of a modified version of this SREB framework and this fourteen step approach will be described as they were applied in 12 colleges over the last six years.


# Proposed Conceptual Schemes

Until the early 1970s, most faculty evaluation schemes in higher education lacked a systematic or comprehensive approach to faculty evaluation. Most faculty evaluations were conducted by the department chairman, with the better systems making some use of data gathered from a formal student rating system, while others used no data at all. Staff evaluation systems were of a similar nature, with the employee's supervisor conducting the annual review, perhaps with the help of a self-rating instrument completed during an interview by the employer and the employee for discussion purposes.

In the 1970s, however, there was a dramatic shift to more comprehensive and systematically planned faculty and staff evaluation systems in universities and colleges. Many of these systems were developed from the assumption and guidelines summarized by Miller in 1972. Miller believed that any system of faculty evaluation should seriously consider beginning with the formulation of basic assumptions. The faculty evaluation model he recommended proceeded from the following six assumptions: 1. the trend toward accountability will continue, 2. merit evaluation is preferable to a seniority system, 3. overall faculty evaluation is inevitable, 4. every evaluation system can be improved, 5. professional development should be available to every faculty member who is evaluated, and 6. faculty evaluation should be for both advancement decisions and faculty development (Miller, 1972, pp. 4-12).

From these assumptions and a related set of principles, Miller developed a model for the evaluation of teaching that contained a broader view of the role of the college teacher than we have had in the past. Previously, the teacher's role had been conceptualized in terms of research, teaching, service, and professional activities. Miller (1972, p. 21) pointed out that college teachers were engaging in a much wider range of activities than in the past. For this reason, he felt that the following categories should be used in describing and evaluating college teaching: classroom teaching, advising, faculty service and relations, management (administration), performing and visual arts, professional services, publications, public service, and research.

Under this system the faculty member entered into an annual performance contract with his or her department chairperson. Miller (1972, p. 80) argued that such a contracting process would lead to the establishment of tasks and the selection of evaluation criteria that would best reflect the nature of the institution, the needs and direction of the department, and the interests and abilities of the faculty member. Miller then described a variety of procedures that could be used to collect data from a variety of sources such as students, faculty colleagues, and administrators in each of his proposed nine evaluation categories. Finally, he showed how these data could be employed to calculate an overall performance rating for a staff member (Smith, 1976).

Since Miller's presentation, a number of other conceptual schemes too numerous to mention have been proposed for higher education staff evaluation programs (Centra, 1979; North and Scholl, 1978; Seldin, 1980, 1984; Smith, 1976, 1983; Southern Regional Education Board, 1977). Each of these proposed evaluation schemes has recommended a systematic and comprehensive approach to faculty evaluation. The proponents of these programs have also suggested the need for multiple data-based evaluation programs. Of these systems, which have focused primarily on faculty evaluation, the author has found the Southern Regional Education Board's conceptual framework to be of most value in helping colleges design new or revised faculty and staff evaluation programs.

## Southern Regional Education Board's Framework for Faculty Evaluation

As a result of the SREB's survey and case study research (Southern Regional Education Board, 1977, p. 31), four separate components of systematic faculty evaluation programs were identified. The four components of the SREB "Framework for Developing the Components of a Systematic Faculty Evaluation Program" are as follows:

1. Purpose. Objectives and desired outcomes of the program.
2. Areas. Evaluation areas are those functions or attributes to be examined teaching, research, service, and so on.
3. Elements. Essential elements of evaluation are: Criteria specific attainments subsumed under each area; Standards attainment levels expected for each criterion; Evidence data or information for determining level attained, and how the data are to be compiled.
4. Procedures. Sequence of activities for making personnel decisions, assisting with development or improvement, or carrying out other purposes.

This framework was used in the SREB's 1977-79 Faculty Evaluation Project (Southern Regional Education Board, 1979). For two years, this project promoted principles of comprehensive, systematic faculty and staff evaluation. During an eighteen-month period, this project worked closely with thirty institutions including nine two-year colleges, to assist them in developing such programs.

The step-by-step application of the SREB framework proved to be highly successful in helping two-year and four-year colleges improve their faculty evaluation programs. Of the nine two-year colleges in this project, eight were judged by a team of three evaluators to have a high or medium probability of achieving positive and permanent changes in their faculty evaluation programs (Southern Regional Education Board, 1979). One of the nine colleges in this project that successfully applied the SREB model to its faculty evaluation program was Jackson State Community College (Jackson State Community College, 1979).

Robert Harrell (1980) Dean of Academic Affairs at Jackson State, has described the concepts which he felt were

fundamental to Jackson State's successful revision of its
faculty evaluation program. These concepts were:
  1. Faculty are evaluated in areas for which they have a
     principle responsibility.
  2. Multiple evaluators or sources of evaluation are utilized.
  3. Evaluators evaluate those areas of faculty responsibility
     for which they have appropriate expertise.
  4. Faculty members develop individualized evaluation
     programs.
  5. Evaluation outcomes or evaluation results for each area of
     responsibility are expressed no more definitely than as one
     of three possible levels of performance.
  6. The level of performance is determined by a criterion-
     referenced approach to evaluation.
  7. Formative and summative evaluation procedures are
     included in the evaluation process.
  8. Faculty evaluation is a dynamic and ongoing process.

Harrell believes these concepts may be applied directly or
may be adaptable for effective use in other institutions, but
only if such concepts are consistent with institutional mission
and goals.

At Jackson State Community College (JSCC), formative, or
ongoing, evaluation provides information for professional
growth and development. Summative evaluations at JSCC
provide information for personnel decisions with respect to
promotion, tenure, and salary decisions. Faculty and staff are
evaluated in each of their areas of responsibility with the
following terms: needs improvement, expected performance,
and exceptional performance. The JSCC program of staff
evaluation provides an excellent model for two-year college
staffs that wish to improve their personal evaluation systems.
It is also a very good example of the effectiveness of the SREB
conceptual framework for faculty evaluation. The four-year
college and university evaluation programs developed in the
SREB project provide other examples of excellent models for

these types of institutions (Southern Regional Education Board, 1979).

## Finding a Conceptual Framework for Staff Evaluation

To date, most colleges have focused their evaluation efforts on the development of improved full-time faculty evaluation systems. Such efforts have often neglected other equally important personnel groups, such as administrators, part-time faculty, academic support staff, and so on. Because of the equally valuable contributions these groups make to the college program, there is likely to be an increasing emphasis on staff as opposed to faculty evaluation in the next five to ten years. This will be an appropriate shift of emphasis for two reasons. First, in a time of declining resources, student enrollments and full-time staff, the contributions of each employee become increasingly vital to the success of a college program. In the latter half of the 1980s and in the 1990s, colleges and college employees will have to learn to do more with less. This means that each employee's contribution to the total educational program will increase in importance over the next decade. Second, the shift to staff evaluation should enhance employee morale, job satisfaction, and staff productivity. Evaluation should enable employees to see ways to grow without leaving their current jobs. This should be a healthy development in a profession where there is currently little opportunity for job mobility either externally or internally.

One college, Central Piedmont Community College (CPCC), has already developed its system for staff evaluation. The purpose of this system, which appears to be working very well, is to "encourage all personnel to aspire to higher levels of performance in the service of students, the community, and the institution." (Cheshire and Hagemeyer, 1981-82, p. 34). The objectives of this program are 1. to identify standards against which each employee's performance can be measured, 2. to identify individuals who are performing at a satisfactory level, 3. to provide assurance and encouragement to individuals who are performing at a satisfactory level, and 4. to identify and assist individuals whose performance needs significant improvement.

One of the keys to the success of this system appears to be the high level of administrative support for the program. A second important factor is the extensive involvement of employees in the development and pilot testing of new evaluation instruments. As a result of this process, the original objective of a campus-wide evaluation plan has been achieved. However, instead of having one evaluation form for everyone, CPCC has many instruments, each measuring the performance of specific tasks or jobs.

The Central Piedmont system, with its annual reviews and ratings, appears to contain all of the components proposed in the previously discussed SREB conceptual framework for developing a faculty evaluation program. First, the purposes were clearly defined as the first steps in the development of a new system. Second, the areas of evaluation were identified for each major employee group. Third, criteria and standards were set, with ratings then made by both the employees and the supervisors. Finally, procedures were outlined which called for an annual performance review of self- and supervisory ratings and the placement of an evaluation summary in the employee's personnel file (Cheshire and Hagemeyer, 1981-82).

It would appear that the SREB framework can be applied as a very useful conceptual framework for the broader area of staff evaluation. The strongest support for this position comes from the University of Florida (UF) National Faculty Evaluation Project for Community and Junior Colleges. This six-year project began in June 1980 under the sponsorship of the university's Institute of Higher Education. The purpose of this project was to assist two-year and four-year colleges in the improvement of their faculty or staff evaluation systems. A second major purpose was to test the usefulness of the SREB conceptual framework and approach to helping colleges improve their evaluation programs. The first eight colleges in this project that participated were Arapahoe Community College (Littleton, Colo.), Gateway Technical Institute (Racine, Wis.), Mountain Empire Community College (Big Stone Gap, Va.), Moraine Valley Community College (Palos Hills, Ill.), Mohawk Valley Community College (Utica, N.Y.), Patrick Henry Community College (Martinsville, Va.), Rockingham Community College (Wentworth, N.C.) and the University College of the University of Cincinnati (Cincinnati, Ohio).

Under this new program, the participating colleges agreed to send a team of three faculty and one top-level administrator to Gainesville, Florida, each summer for a three-day workshop on faculty evaluation and development. In the first workshop, the participants were introduced to the SREB conceptual framework for faculty evaluation and were given a variety of other resource materials on how to plan for a new or revised faculty evaluation program. In the second workshop, conducted in 1981, the teams received additional instruction on how to implement their new plans. In 1982, the workshop focused on how the colleges could evaluate the impact of their new programs. This last workshop also focused on how the colleges could establish viable faculty development programs to complement their new faculty evaluation efforts.

In addition to the summer workshops, this project has involved the extensive use of University of Florida staff members and external resource consultants. As part of the project, each team was required to have a one-day progress evaluation visit by a University of Florida staff member. These visits were conducted during the winter months of each year and have been very useful. Each team was also encouraged to

employ non-University of Florida consultants for at least one
day during each of the project's three years. These visits have
also been helpful, with the consultants serving as external
change agents to the college.

This project met its objectives. Each of the eight colleges
developed and implemented a new or revised faculty and/or
staff evaluation plan using the SREB "Framework for
Developing the Components of a Systematic Faculty
Evaluation Program." Because of the success of the project,
four new colleges were added to this program in 1983. These
colleges were Beaufort Technical College (Beaufort, S.C.), J.
Sargeant Reynolds Community College (Richmond, Va.),
Olympic College (Bremerton, Wa.), and Palm Beach Junior
College (Palm Beach, Fl.). The successes of these last four
colleges and some of the unique aspects of their new or revised
faculty evaluation schemes will be discussed in a later section
of this chapter. These four colleges have just completed the full
implementation of their new programs. A third three year
project for colleges, universities, and/or departments wishing
to make changes in their faculty evaluation programs is
planned for 1987-1990. Applications for this program are still
being accepted through the University of Florida's Institute of
Higher Education.

One of the interesting findings of this project is that the
SREB conceptual framework can be applied effectively in the
development of staff evaluation as well as the faculty
evaluation system. One of the colleges in this project,
Arapahoe Community College, has employed the SREB model
to develop a comprehensive and systematic staff evaluation
program for all of its employees. Another project college,
Rockingham Community College, has taken a similar
approach. Readers wishing more information on these new
programs should contact the respective college presidents or
deans or the University of Florida's Institute of Higher
Education.

# FOURTEEN STEP STRATEGY FOR SUCCESS

This section was written for faculty, administrators, and other staff members that are dissatisfied with their current faculty/staff evaluation system(s). This section outlines the steps that we have found in the Institute of Higher Education at the University of Florida to be most successful in the development of improved faculty evaluation programs.

## Preliminary Activities

### Support for the Project

The development of a new or revised evaluation is a major institutional undertaking which will require adequate financial and administrative support. Both the Florida and SREB projects found that the active support and involvement of top-level administrators was central to the successful implementation of a new evaluation program. In order to achieve adequate support it is recommended that:

1. A college task force or team should be appointed by either the college President or Academic Vice President (or Dean) to investigate the need for changes in the college's faculty/ staff evaluation program. This committee should be appointed for a three-year period for the purpose of investigating the need for a new faculty/staff evaluation program at the college and for the purpose of developing, implementing, and evaluation of a new program.

2. This team should be comprised of the following four individuals, i.e., the College Academic Vice-President or Dean, a Department Chairperson and two faculty. Teams can be expanded to five or six members. These individuals should be carefully selected. They should be individuals who have the respect of the faculty, and they should be influential leaders in the college.

3. In addition to being the campus leaders, this campus team or committee should consist of a group of individuals who are willing to put in long hours of hard work both during the academic year and over the summer months. To be successful there will be times when the campus team will need to meet weekly or twice a week to accomplish its task.

4. The college administration must be willing to spend at least $2,000 per year for outside consultant assistance or for the dues to cover membership in the type of project described in this chapter. The use of internal and/or external consultants as change agents is essential to the successful revision of an evaluation program. The consultant serves as an important source of current information as well as someone who can provide an objective view that will keep the project moving to its end.

5. Financial resources should also be set aside for travel for the campus team or evaluation committee. Approximately $2,000 to $2,500 will be needed for a team of four individuals to attend conferences or workshops on evaluation or to visit colleges where successful faculty evaluation programs have been implemented. (If these funds are not used for travel, then they will probably be needed to cover released time for one or more of the committee members at critical times over the project's three year duration.)

6. The college should also set aside approximately $500-$1000 a year for the purchase of evaluation materials. Quite frequently these funds will be needed to purchase a software package for a computerized student rating instrument or to cover the cost of purchasing and processing completed student rating instruments.

The active support and involvement of top-level administrators is a must, if not the most, important component factor in establishing a new or revised faculty/staff evaluation program. University of Florida project institutions at which the President and Academic Vice President early voiced their support, strongly communicated a sense of need for change, and actively participated in the development of the new system have been, without exception, those colleges where positive change has taken place most effectively. A college team or committee that feels it does not have the support of its administration should work to get that support before taking any steps to revise and improve a faculty/staff evaluation system.

## Major Factors That Will Help or Hinder a Team or Committee's Progress

In addition to making sure that the college has committed the necessary financial resources, approximately $15,000 over a three year period, to make this project a success, the campus team must also check on some other factors before starting its work. These factors, while not as important as the elements of administrative and financial support, will also determine whether or not a successful change is possible. Both the SREB and the University of Florida projects have found that the following institutional characteristics, in descending order of importance, are important if change in faculty/staff evaluation programs are to take place.

1. Faculty and/or staff involvement throughout the project. The faculty/staff must be involved in all phases of the development of the program. The campus team will need to educate the faculty/staff regarding alternative evaluation programs and involve them in the decision making process over a three year period. At any given time, the faculty/staff should feel that their views have been adequately considered in the new design and that the finished product was a result of primarily their efforts.
2. Faculty/staff trust in administration. The campus team must work to develop this trust if it does not exist when a

decision is made to change the current faculty/staff evaluation system. Changes in faculty/staff evaluation programs are more likely to be positively received by the faculty/staff when the administration is viewed as responsive to their interests. This trust can be developed by the administration taking an active listening role in the change process and by incorporating faculty/staff input into involving new plans.

3. Faculty/staff dissatisfaction with status quo. In the early months of the revision process, the campus team should determine the level of dissatisfaction with current faculty evaluation plans or components of those plans. The greater the dissatisfaction the less resistance there will be to proposals for change. Unless 50% or more of the faculty and/or staff are dissatisfied with the present evaluation system, it is unlikely that a proposal for a new evaluation plan will be accepted.

4. Historical acceptance of faculty evaluation. Campus evaluation teams or committees formed in colleges that have had limited or no experience with faculty/staff evaluation can expect greater resistance to their efforts to develop such an evaluation. Until a campus faculty/staff can see some value in a sound evaluation program, they will resist organizational change in this area. Colleges that have had evaluation programs in the past will face less resistance to change.

5. Presence of an institutional statement covering the philosophy and uses of evaluation. A clear sense of purpose is critical to any faculty/staff evaluation plan. This can come in the form of a board policy or a statement of the objectives of a new faculty/staff evaluation plan. The preparation of this statement, if it does not already exist within the college, will be one of the first tasks of the evaluation team or committee.

6. Degree of centralized institutional decision making. New

evaluation policies and procedures will be harder to develop in universities, colleges and/or departments characterized by decentralized decision-making authority (i.e., a concentration of power at the president, dean or department chairman levels). Large universities with fairly autonomous decision making at the department level will have greater difficulty achieving faculty acceptance of a university-wide or standardized approach to faculty evaluation. At such larger colleges and universities plans will be best developed at the college and/or department level under some general institution-wide guidelines.

For purposes of this section the above characteristics should be considered a checklist of "readiness factors." Colleges and universities with all or most of these factors are likely to make the greatest progress in improving their faculty/staff evaluation programs. A newly appointed campus team should determine their college's "readiness" for change before designing a new or revised evaluation system. Later in this chapter there will be a discussion of how this can be done.

## A Strategy for Success —
## A Fourteen Step Approach

Outlined below are the steps and time frame being recommended for the successful development of a comprehensive faculty/staff evaluation program.

**First Year**

During the first year, the campus team should take the following steps.

First Month

1. Step One — Become familiar with the literature and research on faculty/staff evaluation by reading the following publications:

   Centra, John, ed. *Determining Faculty Effectiveness*. San

Francisco: Jossey-Bass, Inc., Publishers, 1978.

Miller, Richard I. *Evaluation Faculty Performance.* San Francisco: Jossey-Bass, Inc., Publishers, 1972.

Seldin, P. *Changing Practices in Faculty Evaluation.* San Francisco: Jossey-Bass Publishers, Inc., 1984.

Southern Regional Education Board (SREB) *Improving Faculty Evaluation: A Trial in Strategy.* Atlanta: SREB, 1979.

Second Month

2. Step Two — Employ a consultant to make a presentation to your faculty and staff on the various approaches that are available for faculty/staff evaluation.

Ideally this consultant should describe how the faculty/staff could develop a comprehensive faculty/staff evaluation program. After this presentation, the faculty should be asked to read the following article on Miller's (1972) book.

Arreola, Raoul "Strategy for Developing a Comprehensive Faculty Evaluation System" *Engineering Education.* December, 1979. 239-244.

The faculty would be told at this first meeting with the consultant and team as a result of this activity and their reading of this article, the team was planning to conduct a survey of faculty/staff interests and needs. The purpose of this survey would be to involve the faculty in the development of a new and/or revised faculty/staff evaluation system. The team should also tell the faculty at this point that they have three major objectives. The team should also share that their objectives and time frame at this point are to: 1. develop with the help of the faculty/staff an evaluation system over the next six months, 2. pilot test the new system, after achieving faculty/staff approval of the new plan, in the next academic year, and 3. revise and fully implement the new evaluation program during the third year of the committee's work.

Third and Fourth Month

3. Step Three — Develop a questionnaire to survey the faculty/staff. The purpose of this survey(s) would be to determine: 1. the faculty roles or areas for evaluation, 2. the weights that should be attached to these roles or areas for evaluation purposes, 3. the sources of information that should be used in evaluating these areas, and 4. the weight (%) that should be attached to each source of information for each evaluation category or area.

Once the data has been gathered from the faculty and staff with this instrument, the campus team should tabulate the responses to the faculty for their review and study. The team can then use the results of this survey to develop the first draft of their new evaluation program.

Please note that it will be necessary to develop a different survey questionnaire for each staff group within the institution, i.e., librarians, counselors, non-academic support staff, etc. These questionnaires will require different wording than the wording found in the Faculty survey and will necessitate different role categories. However, all groups will still be asked to indicate the weight (%) they wish to give to the various areas and sources of information in their plan.

Fifth Month

4. Step Four — Develop the first draft of an evaluation plan for each college group using the results of the faculty and staff surveys.

Sixth Month

5. Step Five — Involves sharing the first draft of the committee or team's proposed evaluation package with the college's faculty and staff. This is best done in one large college meeting with all faculty present or in 4 or 5 department or division meetings. In this meeting(s), the team should take whatever time is necessary, usually 1-2 hours, to carefully explain the proposed faculty evaluation

system. Each faculty member should be given a copy of the plan and then carefully walk through the plan on a page by page basis.

At this stage of development, it is also recommended that the college team make use of a consultant to help them explain their new system to the faculty/staff. This will take some of the heat off the faculty evaluation team and provide for a more objective discussion of the pros and cons of the new system. The consultant can also be useful in citing research to support the committee's new plan. The committee should carefully point out how the plan has been developed using the data from its previous faculty/ staff surveys.

The evaluation committee should expect to get negative reactions and suggestions for improving their plan at this meeting. They should take the position that they welcome these comments and plan to make revisions in their plan. After this meeting the committee should try to make all the necessary revisions suggested before circulating the plan to the faculty for additional faculty reaction.

Seventh through Eleventh Months

6. Step Six — Prepare for Pilot Testing the New Faculty/Staff Evaluation Programs.

After the evaluation plan has been thoroughly reviewed, revised, and thoroughly discussed in the college, the evaluation committee or team should prepare a pilot testing program for the new system(s). The assumption is made here that the faculty and staff by now feel fairly comfortable with the new program and that they are willing to let the faculty/staff committee proceed with a pilot test during the next academic year. In preparing for this pilot test, the team should do the following over this two month period:

a. Ask for a group of volunteers to pilot test the new system(s). Here the team should work to get volunteers for the pilot test from every department and from every employed group affected by the new plan.

b. Once a group of volunteers has been identified the team should develop and order enough evaluation packages and evaluation instruments for the pilot test. This would include making sure the college has made all of the necessary arrangements for the printing, scoring and giving back of student rating instruments or other commercially prepared materials that might be a part of the new system.

Twelfth Month

7. Step Seven — Meet with College Faculty, Pilot Test Group and College Department Chairs and Deans to Prepare them for the Pilot Test.

This part of the program is probably best done during the month of August after the college faculty and staff have returned from their summer vacations to start the new academic year, the second year of this faculty evaluation project. Time should be set aside prior to classes for an all college faculty meeting, department or division meetings, and for meetings with the various other staff groups that are to be evaluated under the new plan. The purpose of these meetings should be: 1. to inform the faculty of the evaluation team's or committee's progress and 2. explain how the pilot test will be conducted during the academic year. At these meetings faculty and staff should be given another copy of the proposed new faculty/staff evaluation system just in case they have not seen or had a chance to react to the team's latest draft.

A special meeting should then be held prior to classes with all administrators who will be involved in the pilot test. The purpose of this meeting will be to fully explain and walk the administrators through the new program. Department heads, directors and supervisors, and the evaluators, will be the key persons in determining the successful or failure of the new system both in the pilot study and in the future. (The team may even want to consider having a summer workshop with this group with an outside consultant present to assist in the training of the department chairs and directors for their new roles).

After the administrators have met, another meeting should be held for all administrators, faculty and staff members that will be involved in the pilot program. The purpose of this meeting will be to fully explain the new program to this volunteer group, walking them through each aspect of the proposed new evaluation plan. In preparation for this meeting, the evaluation team or committee should prepare a sample set of papers for a hypothetical faculty or staff member who has gone through the system. The more concrete examples the evaluation team can give the faculty as to how all system documents and reports are to be prepared, the more success the team is likely to have with individuals in the pilot test.

If the pilot test involves the use of peer review committees, then these committees should also be established at this time. These committees should also have a workshop to receive special training in their role in the evaluation process.

## Summary

This section contains an outline of the essential steps for a faculty evaluation team or committee to follow during its first year of new program development.

Little has been said in this section about the selection of a sound student rating system. A common error made by evaluation committees charged with developing a faculty evaluation program is to begin by designing a student rating form or student evaluation questionnaire. Although student ratings of faculty performance are an important component of a comprehensive faculty evaluation system, they are by no means the only, or even necessarily the most important component. We have tried to suggest here and in the next chapter that there is a better way to go about designing and developing a faculty and/or staff evaluation program.

Individuals or campus teams wishing more information on student rating instruments should review the appendix on this subject found in Centra (1978) book. This appendix contains information on the nature, cost, etc. of 12 different student rating forms. A college committee or team should let its faculty select a student rating instrument from two or three questionnaires which the committee feels most effectively meets the needs of their particular faculty or faculty groups. This way the faculty will feel that they have had some voice in selecting a rating form.

The development of a comprehensive faculty evaluation system has been found to involve a considerable amount of "political" groundwork if the resulting system is to be successful. That is, attention must be paid to the need to systematically involve faculty and other appropriate interested groups in the design of the evaluation procedure. This involvement cannot simply take the form of faculty committees or task forces although such bodies are necessary to implement the steps involved in the design of the system. In a very real sense faculty must be involved in the actual design specification of the faculty evaluation program. Listed below are some additional steps which have been found to be successful in incorporating faculty values and input into the overall design of the system. Such input is critical if the faculty evaluation program which is developed is to be accepted by the faculty. The following is an overview and summary of some other steps the faculty evaluation team would need to take during its first year of operation. This list of steps was developed by Arreola (1979) for our first faculty evaluation project.

Step 1: Determine the faculty role model of the institution. That is, determine which of the many activities faculty engage in should be evaluated.

Step 2: Determine how much value or "weight" should be placed on each role in the faculty role model. That is, establish the relative importance or priorities of each role in the institution as a whole (including faculty and the administration).

Step 3: Define each role in terms of readily observable or documentable achievements, projects, or performances. That is, clearly establish what "evidence" will be acceptable in evaluating faculty performance.

Step 4: Determine which source or sources should provide the information on which the evaluation of each role will be based. That is, clearly establish from whom information will be gathered in preparing the "evidence" to be used in the evaluation process.

Step 5: Determine how much value or "weight" should be placed on information provided by the various selected sources for each role. That is, clearly establish how much impact the information from a given source will have on the evaluation of a faculty member's performance.

Step 6: Determine how the information from the various sources should be gathered. That is, given the type of information that is to be gathered and the sources from which it is to be gathered, determine the best mechanism for gathering it (i.e. questionnaire, interview schedule, checklist, peer review panel, etc.).

Step 7: Design or select appropriate forms, questionnaire, procedures and protocols necessary to gather the specified information.

## Pilot Testing, Implementing and Evaluating
## The New Plan — The Second and Third Year

The assumption is made in this section that the college evaluation team or committee is now ready to begin its pilot test. This part covers the steps that the evaluation team should follow during the pilot testing phase as well as during the full-implementation and evaluation of its new plan.

Thirteenth through Seventeenth Month

8. Step Eight — Assisting and Evaluating Faculty or Staff Member Goal Setting Conferences with Their Department/Division Chairs or Immediate Supervisors.

Most faculty/staff evaluation plans are likely to contain a goal setting conference for each new employment period. These conferences are usually held at the end of an academic year, after the faculty member has been evaluated, so that new goals and objectives in the areas of research training, service, etc. can be set for the coming year. In a pilot study these goal and weight setting conferences are likely to take place either in the spring of the previous academic year or in the early fall of the new academic year. To assist in these conferences, the college evaluation team or committee should notify all department chairs/supervisors when it is time to conduct these conferences. The chairs and supervisors in turn should then notify all individuals in the pilot study that it is time for them to prepare their annual evaluation and development objectives.

After the goal setting conferences have been completed, the faculty/staff evaluation committee should review the goals and objectives that have been left with each supervisor. They should also interview a number of the department chairs and faculty to determine whether or not the pilot conferences are being conducted according to their expectations. In addition to interviewing some of the pilot participants at this stage, the team may want to meet with

all the pilot test supervisors and then all of the pilot test
faculty/staff to get their impressions of, suggestions for,
and reactions to the pilot test conferences.

Thirteen through Eighteen Months

9. Step Nine — Assisting and Evaluating through Pilot
   Study's Use of a Student Rating Instrument
   Most faculty evaluation systems are likely to have as part
   of their new evaluation system a student rating
   instrument. The evaluation committee should make sure
   the administration and use of this instrument is done
   properly and according to the guidelines in their newly
   proposed evaluation system. Mistakes or delays made in
   the administration or student rating instruments or in the
   return of student rating data to faculty can quickly kill any
   new faculty evaluation plan. The faculty evaluation team
   should make sure that the agency supplying and scoring
   the student rating instrument can deliver results on the
   dates specified by the committee for both pilot test and for
   future administrations of the student rating instrument.
   In this pilot test, student rating data should be collected
   both in the Fall and Winter terms of the pilot test, if
   possible. After the first administration and feedback of
   student ratings to the pilot faculty, the evaluation team
   should meet with the pilot test faculty and department
   chairs to see if there were any problems with this aspect of
   the program.

Nineteenth through Twentieth Month

10. Step Ten — Assisting and Evaluating the Pilot Test of the
    Peer Evaluation Component
    A new faculty/staff evaluation system may or may not
    have a peer evaluation component. If it does, then the
    evaluation team will need to carefully train the peer review
    committees for their work. This will require a special
    workshop prior to the faculty members submission of
    his/her annual report or part of that annual report to

his/her department or college peer evaluation committee. In addition to this workshop, the evaluation team should make sure the pilot faculty/staff members follow a uniform format in submitting their materials and/or reports to the peer review committees. Uniform procedures and standard review practices in this area will help to assure reliable and valid peer ratings. After the peer review teams have completed their work, the evaluation committee/team should meet with these teams to determine their suggestions for improving the system.

Nineteenth through Twentieth Month

11. Step Eleven — Assisting and Evaluating the Pilot Testing of Faculty/Staff Member Annual Evaluation Conferences with Their Department Chairs or Immediate Supervisors. At the end of each evaluation period, whether the college has decided on an annual evaluation or more lengthy review period for evaluation, it will be necessary for the evaluator to meet with the evaluatee. After the pilot annual review conferences, the evaluation committee/team should meet with the department chairs and faculty/staff members separately to determine if any problems arose in this final phase of the pilot test. Information from these meetings and other phases of the pilot test can then be used to make any necessary changes in the new evaluation plan(s) prior to full implementation of the program in the next academic year.

Twentieth through Twenty-third Month

12. Step Twelve — Revision of the Faculty/Staff Evaluation Plan for Final Implementation and a Faculty Vote of Approval.

Even after the pilot test the evaluation committee/team should be prepared to make additional changes in their proposed plan prior to a faculty/staff vote. As in the past, the preparation of the proposed plan for another faculty review will probably require a considerable amount of someone's energy and time.

If the evaluation team has involved the faculty and staff in its work throughout the first two years of the project, then there should be a positive institutional climate for approval of the plan(s). The team should circulate its plan to all faculty and staff prior to meeting with all of the faculty and the other staff groups.

Once the evaluation plans have been accepted, the committee/team should have the plan placed in a loose leaf notebook. (A notebook is recommended here so that sections of the plan can be easily changed and pages substituted in faculty/staff notebooks in future years.)

Twenty-Fourth Month

13. Step Thirteen — Preparation of Faculty and Staff for Full Implementation of the Plan(s) During the Third Year of this Project.

    At the Fall college faculty and staff meetings, all members of the college staff should be given their copy of the new evaluation plan in notebook form. Also at this time the evaluation committee/team should once again carefully walk each faculty and staff group through the new plan, taking time to answer any questions staff members might have about the requirements and procedures of the new plan.

Twenty-Fifth through Thirty-Sixth Month

14. Step Fourteen — Full Implementation of the New Evaluation Plan.

    Here the committee/team's task will be to carefully monitor the implementation of its new plan. The committee/team should conduct periodic spot checks in various departments to make sure supervisors and faculty or staff are correctly following the new plan.

    At the end of the 9-12 month full implementation period, the evaluation committee/team should send a brief evaluation survey to all individuals involved in the evaluation process. Responses to this survey will certainly give the evaluation committee/team an indication of how well they have performed their work.

Revisions can be made in the evaluation during the summer months following the first full year of implementation of the new plan. After these revisions are made the college will be ready for its second year of experience with a new evaluation system.

## Summary

This part of the chapter contains an outline of the critical steps in implementing a new faculty/staff evaluation plan. Hopefully, the college, during these three years, will also have developed a new or revised faculty/staff development program to complement the new evaluation program.

## Lessons Learned

As was mentioned earlier, four colleges, i.e., Beaufort Technical College, J. Sargeant Reynolds Community College, Olympic College, and Palm Beach Junior College are just completing their three years in the University of Florida's National Faculty Evaluation project. Described here are some unique aspects of these four new programs that other colleges, wishing to improve their faculty evaluation programs, may want to investigate.

Beaufort Technical College (BTC) has developed a form to evaluate the quality of faculty student advising at this particular institution. Students complete this form after they have seen their faculty advisor and prior to their registration each semester. They are then required to submit their completed rating form as part of the college's registration requirements. (Beaufort Technical College, 1986) Feedback from this form has been very helpful to both the faculty and the college. Half of the evaluation rating form gives the faculty member immediate feedback on the quality of his/her advising each term and the other half of the form provides the college administration with student reactions to the college's student personnel services. Data from this form becomes part of each faculty member's overall performance evaluation since each faculty member must set goals and objectives in the area of advising. (It was interesting to note that while none of our project's first eight colleges included student advising as one of the areas for faculty evaluation, all four of our last set of colleges felt that this was an area of faculty member responsibility that should be evaluated annually). This increased interest in the quality of student advising is no doubt due to the recent concern expressed over declining or stabilizing enrollments and relatively high student dropout rates in some institutions.

Other aspects of the BTC plan include the development of a merit pay system and the evaluation of faculty over the following five areas: Teaching and Instruction, Student Advisement, College Service, Community Service and Professional Development. As the title of the plan indicates, one of its major purposes is for faculty development. Most of the colleges we have worked with have included this as one of the major purposes for their programs. It seems to us that this is a very appropriate step to take since it would be unfair for a college to evaluate its staff and then not provide some resources for individuals for correcting deficiencies.

One final aspect of the Beaufort Technical College plan bears mentioning. The plan only contains administrator, peer, and student evaluations of the faculty member's performance. Self-ratings by the faculty member of his/her performance are not weighted or included as part of the BTC system. We think this is a positive aspect of this program. Too often we have found that self-ratings bias a faculty rating system in favor of the faculty member and they fail to give a totally accurate picture of the faculty member's performance. In recent years we have encouraged colleges not to include self-ratings in their faculty evaluation programs. We have done this because there is a tendency for faculties to want to place a high weight on their own ratings. This quite frequently results in final ratings that do not reflect differences in faculty performance.

J. Sargeant Reynolds Community College (JSRCC) has developed a faculty evaluation system for a multi-campus situation. (J. Sargeant Reynolds Community College, 1986). This college faculty is unionized and is located on three different campuses. While we do not usually recommend that a college attempt to develop their own student rating system, this college has been successful in developing a new student rating system for its faculty. This college has also developed a peer evaluation component as part of its new evaluation plan. We have learned that peer evaluation can be a very controversial part of any new faculty evaluation system and for this reason it is often dropped from a new plan. AT JSRCC however, each faculty member is evaluated by one of his/her peers each year. The faculty member selects the peer, which is probably a weakness of the system, but at least it is a start in the right direction. Each peer reviewer receives a portfolio of material prepared by the faculty member. The peer then rates the faculty member on a scale of 1-5 in the areas of: Teaching, Advising, Professional Growth and Development, College Service, and Community Service.

Perhaps one of the strongest aspects of JSRCC's new plan is its goal setting procedure. Each faculty member is required to meet with his/her Division Chair at the beginning of each academic year to set new objectives for his/her work. These objectives must fit with the college's goals and objectives for the coming academic year. The college's goals are set by the administrative staff, i.e. the President, the Vice-President, and the Deans each year and given to the faculty. This year, because of a rather severe enrollment drop in the previous academic year, the college faculty are writing more goals in the area of student recruitment and retention. We highly recommend this approach to goal setting since it is consistent with much of the theory in business and industry which stresses the importance of achieving a congruence in organizations between organization and individual goals.

One of the major lessons learned at JSRCC is that the revision of a faculty evaluation system often requires a number of compromises between the college administration and faculty. This plan may be unique in that it contains a section on administrator evaluation. The inclusion of an administration evaluation component is a unique aspect of this plan. At first the college administration was opposed to the joining of the faculty evaluation and administrator evaluation plans into one document with similar policies and procedures. However, a compromise was reached and the J. Sargeant Reynolds plan now includes an administrator evaluation plan that allows for a weight of between 30-50% for faculty evaluation of some of the administrators in the college.

We have learned that faculty are more likely to support a new faculty evaluation plan if the administration of the college is also developing an administration evaluation plan that allows for faculty input. We would recommend that colleges develop administrator evaluation plans as they develop or revise their faculty systems. Such parallel activity seems to result in a greater willingness on the part of the faculty to make changes in their own evaluation systems.

Olympic College has developed a Faculty Assessment Handbook (1986) that describes the objectives and central features of their new assessment program. The unique aspect of this plan is that it focuses almost entirely on faculty development. The faculty assessment program is not tied to any annual salary decisions, to merit pay, or to promotion system, although one of the college's four development objectives does indicate that this program is a means of assessing performance of the faculty for the purpose of retention and/or reappointment. Another unique feature of this plan is that the assessment cycle is for a two-year period. In this two-year period, the faculty member sets his/her goals/objectives and then meets periodically for progress reviews. As with many of our other colleges, Olympic College has adopted the Arizona Course/Instructor Evaluation Questionnaire (CIEQ) and is having good success with this student rating instrument. Also, as with many of our other colleges, the faculty at Olympic College are asked to develop a portfolio and self-assessment report during and at the end of the two-year evaluation period. This portfolio and report, which contain examples of the faculty member's accomplishments, become the basis for director decisions regarding faculty member strengths and weaknesses.

The Chairman of the college evaluation team at Olympic College felt that his team was successful in developing a new plan for the following reasons:

1. The team made effective use of outside consultants as change agents. About twice a year the team would bring in a new consultant to introduce the faculty to a new aspect of faculty evaluation or to train division chairs or faculty in the use of new procedures or evaluation instruments.

2. The team met regularly for the three year period and maintained the same membership. This resulted in a sustained effort on the part of a dedicated group of people.

3. The team had an action plan for each of the three years and was always one step ahead of the faculty and administration in its anticipation of staff concerns.

4. The final evaluation plan was greatly simplified from its first draft and from the college's first pilot study. The team felt that many faculty evaluation plans fail because of their complexity. Their advice to others has been to keep such plans as simple as possible; additional sections can always be added in later years.

Finally, the team felt that a definite structure and time schedule was important for a project like this. Without externally imposed deadlines, the team felt that it would have taken them twice as long to complete their new plan.

At the time this chapter was written, Palm Beach Community College, the newest member of the University of Florida's Faculty Evaluation Project, had just completed its second year in the project. Because the college's pilot test of its new system involved only a few faculty members on the college's main campus, the college evaluation team has decided to conduct a second test of its new plan with all of the faculty in 1986-87. The lesson learned in this case was that any test of a new system should have good representation from all segments of the faculty and administration. Without good representation and support from influential faculty members in the pilot testing phase, a new faculty evaluation plan will not have a good chance for adoption by the college faculty or administration. The Palm Beach team learned a great deal from their first pilot test. They should have a new plan to describe by the summer of 1987.

## Concluding Comments

Even with the very comprehensive list of recommendations made in this chapter, there is one major area of staff evaluation that has not been covered. That area is the legal aspects of a staff evaluation program. While space does not permit a full exploration, in closing it should be helpful to mention some of the legal considerations associated with staff evaluation. Thomas (1981) has compiled an extensive list of legal considerations which are offered here for the reader's review. This list should help colleges avoid any legal entanglements that might arise as a result of new or revised staff evaluation plans.

1. The criteria should be developed from a job analysis (job-

related) through content validation procedures.

2. Administration, faculty, and students should be involved in the development of the system.

3. Individuals evaluating job performance should observe employees frequently.

4. Where possible, evaluations should be based on observable job behaviors.

5. Evaluation forms must be written in clear and concise language, including directions and purpose.

6. Evaluations should be conducted and scored under standardized conditions.

7. Evaluators must be trained in use of the instrument.

8. Several evaluation sources are required and their evaluations should be independent.

9. Performance evaluation must be conducted before any personnel decisions can be made.

10. Evaluations should be supported by objective evidence of performance results.

11. Student evaluations with comments about the faculty member must not be summarized. Either all or none of the comments should be made public.

12. Classroom observations by colleagues must follow a list of teaching behaviors known to the faculty member being observed.

13. Self-appraisals must not be used for tenure, promotions and retention decisions.

14. Criteria, standards, and procedures should be communicated to the persons being evaluated.

15. Faculty should be informed of the results of their performance evaluation.

16. The evaluation system must not be discriminatory in intent, application, and results.

This list of legal considerations was developed using the references of Holley (1977), Kaplin (1979), and Seldin (1980). Thomas (1981) was careful to note that this proposed set of guidelines provided no guarantee that an institution following these suggestions would not be found liable in a court suit. However, she felt that the probability of such an outcome would be considerably reduced if these guidelines were followed.

It is always dangerous to make predictions about the future, particularly in uncertain times. However, when predictions are based on past experience there is often less chance for error. In closing, the following predictions are offered regarding staff evaluation in college and universities. These predictions are based on the content of this publication and the author's experiences with two major projects on faculty and staff evaluation. These predictions will be of value to colleges considering changes in staff evaluation programs.

1. Successful changes in staff evaluation programs will only occur in those colleges where the institution's President or Chief Academic Officer shows strong administrative support for a new or revised evaluation plan.
2. Effective and long lasting changes in staff evaluation programs will only be found in those two-year colleges where there has been full and extensive staff involvement in the proposed change.
3. The most successful staff evaluation programs will be found in those colleges that develop a base of expertise, both internal and external to the institution, for revising their staff evaluation programs.
4. Change in present staff evaluation programs will only occur at those institutions where there is a generally recognized need for a new or revised evaluation program.
5. Interest in staff evaluation programs will increase in the 1990's with colleges developing staff evaluation plans that cover all employees, not just the faculty.
6. Collective bargaining agreements will not hinder and may even foster, the development of new or revised faculty and staff evaluation and development programs in future

years. Such programs will be found in equal numbers in both unionized and nonunionized colleges.

7. Research and evaluation studies in this area will focus more on the impact of these programs than they have in the past. Little is really known about the impact of staff evaluation procedures on faculty, administrators, part-time faculty, academic support staff, and nonacademic support staff.

Overall, staff evaluation promises to continue to attract considerable attention in the 1980s. This attention will be most appropriate given the central value of this administrative function. The colleges that can most effectively manage, develop, and reward their most important and valuable resource, their staff members, are likely to be the most successful colleges in meeting their educational goals for the remainder of this decade.

# SUMMARY

This chapter, after a review of this historical and conceptual developments of faculty evaluation programs, recommends the adoption of the Southern Regional Education Board's (SREB's) conceptual "Framework Program" in the design of staff evaluation systems. This conceptual scheme is described and its use in the University of Florida's 1980-86 National Faculty Evaluation Project for Colleges and Universities is discussed. The four basic components of the SREB model are: 1. the purpose of the evaluation system; 2. the areas of evaluation; 3. the essential elements of the system standards, criteria, and sources of data; and 4. the procedure to be followed. Subsequent sections contain additional illustrations of how these components have been incorporated into faculty evaluation programs and how a 14 step strategy can be used successfully by colleges, universities, and departments to improve their faculty evaluation programs.

# REFERENCES

Arapahoe Community College. "A Tentative Plan: Arapahoe Community College Handbook on Evaluations and Development." Littleton, Colo: Arapahoe Community College, 1982.

Arreola, R. "Strategy for Developing a Comprehensive Faculty Evaluation System," *Engineering Education*. December, 1979. 239-244.

Beaufort Technical College, "Faculty Development Evaluation System," Beaufort, S.C.: Beaufort Technical College, 1986.

Boyd, J.E., and Schietinger, E.F. *Faculty Evaluation Procedures in Southern Colleges and Universities*. Atlanta, Ga.: Southern Regional Education Board, 1976.

Burks, T., Dziech, B., Hartleb, D., and Langen, D. "A System for Evaluation Teaching Effectiveness." Cincinnati: University College University of Cincinnati, 1982.

Centra, J.A. *Determining Faculty Effectiveness*. San Francisco: Jossey-Bass, 1979.

Cheshire, N., and Hagemeyer, R.H. "Evaluating Job Performance," *Community and Junior College Journal*, December/January 1981-82, 52 (4), 34-37.

Harrell, R.A. "Conceptual Framework for Faculty Evaluation and Faculty Development System at Jackson State Community College." Unpublished paper, Jackson State Community College, 1980.

Holley, W.H., and Field, H.S., "The Law and Performance Evaluation in Education: A Review of Court Cases and Implications for Use." *Journal of Law and Education,* 1977, 6 (4), 427-448.

J. Sargeant Reynolds Community College. "Evaluation and Reward Plan for Personnel Holding Faculty Rank." Richmond, Va.: JSRCC, 1986.

Jackson State Community College. "Manual of Procedures for Faculty Evaluation and Faculty Development System." Jackson, Tenn.: Jackson State Community College, 1979.

Kaplin, W.A. *The Law of Higher Education*. San Francisco: Jossey-Bass, 1979.

Miller, R.I. *Evaluating Faculty Performance,* San Francisco: Jossey-Bass, 1972.

Mills, K.H. "Procedures for the Evaluation of the Instructional Staff." Kenosha, Wis.: Gateway Technical Institute, 1981.

Mohawk Valley Community College, "Evaluation Plan." Utica, N.Y. Mohawk Valley Community College, 1982.

Moraine Valley Community College. "Faculty Evaluation." Palos Hills, Ill.: Moraine Valley Community College, 1982.

Mountain Empire Community College. "Proposed Policy and Procedures for the Evaluation of Faculty at Mountain Empire Community College." Big Stone Gap, Va.: Mountain Empire Community College, 1982.

North, J., and Scholl, S. *Revising a Faculty Evaluation System: A Workbook for Decision Makers*. Washingon, D.C.: 1978.

Olympic College. "Faculty Assessment Handbook," Bremerton, Washington: Olympic College, 1986.

Patrick Henry Community College. "Faculty Evaluation Plan." Martinsville, Va.: Patrick Henry Community College, 1982.

Rockingham Community College. "Evaluation Plan." Wentworth, N.C.: Rockingham Community College, 1982.

Seldin, P. *Successful Faculty Evaluation Programs*. Crugers, N.Y.: Coventry Press, 1980.

Seldin, P. *Changing Practices in Faculty Evaluation*. San Francisco, California: Jossey-Bass, 1984.

Smith, A.B. *Faculty Development and Evaluation in Higher Education*. ERIC/Higher Education Report, 8. Washington, D.C.: American Association for Higher Education, 1976.

Smith, A.B., Editor, *Evaluating Faculty and Staff: New Directions for Community Colleges* (No. 41). San Francisco: Jossey-Bass, March, 1983.

Southern Regional Education Board. *Improving Faculty Evaluation: A Trial in Strategy*. Atlanta, Ga.: Southern Regional Educational Board, 1979.

Southern Regional Education Board. *Faculty Evaluation for Improved Learning*. Atlanta, Ga.: Southern Regional Education Board, 1977.

Thomas, W.E. "Legal Considerations." Paper presented at the American Association of Community and Junior Colleges Conference, Washington, D.C., April 1981.

# Continuing Education: Directions and Implications

Brian Donnelly
Sheryl Schoen-Poole

## INTRODUCTION

Continuing Education efforts are major programs at many colleges and universities. What continuing education programs mean and what impacts they have in and on their respective institutions vary widely.

The degree of impact on the institutional budget, the curriculum, the faculty, or the relationship to the community is related to how a program is defined and the purposes and

**Brian L. Donnelly,** Ph.D., is a past President of the National Council on Community Services and Continuing Education, and a member of the Board of Directors for the American Association of Community and Junior Colleges. Dr. Donnelly holds the Ph.D. from Michigan State University, the M.A. from Notre Dame and the B.S. from Boston College. Dr. Donnelly is past President of Fisher Junior College in Boston.

**Sheryl Schoen-Poole,** M.A., received her Masters Degree from the University of Vermont. She is the former Coordinator of Admissions at the University of Vermont and a recent Executive Assistant and Coordinator of Continuing Education Special Programs at Fisher Junior College.

expectations of the college leadership for it. For example, a continuing education program may be regarded as a necessary expense in linking the institution to the community the college serves; or it may be expected to generate a profit and contribute to the quasi-endowment of the institution; or it may be seen as fundamental to meeting the educational purposes of the institution by creating educational access for new target populations. In any case, the range of expectations and meanings for continuing education programs from non-credit, arbitrary, leisure-time programs to traditional credit instruction for adult full-time and part-time learners offered on or off campus has sometimes led to institutional confusion.

The confusion has come in part from the different approaches the different constituents have held for continuing education. Pragmatic economic needs, deep-seated educational convictions, or laissez-faire administrative approaches to development have provided different bases for expanding the role of higher educational institutions in building programs and activities aimed at adult learners over the past twenty years. Regardless of whether or how the continuing education efforts were defined, there have been impacts by continuing education programs on the college as a whole. The review of internal and external institutional factors and conditions can help colleges lay a groundwork for clear continuing education outcomes and expectations for agreed upon impacts on the college as a whole.

While Brookfield (*Understanding and Facilitating Adult Learning*) and Heerman, *et al.* (*New Directions for Community Colleges: Serving Lifelong Learners*) have discussed the impact of institutions on continuing education programs and the major elements in a two-year college continuing education program respectively, there is an absence of discussion of the impact of continuing education programs on the institution. As the outreach area of many institutions, the continuing education operation often has significant impact on the budget, shape and direction of the college.

The demographic and economic constraints of diminished potential traditional age students and higher operating costs have led many college leaders in both the public and private sectors to the development and implementation of continuing education programs with the hope of generating profits to support general costs of operating the college. The programs have not always been well thought out, nor have the levels of commitment always been even. The impacts of continuing education programs on their respective colleges and universities have varied.

This chapter will contain an analysis of continuing education program definitions, purposes and a consideration of some pragmatic issues when there is institutional confusion about the meaning of continuing education and expectations from it; an identification and analysis of the factors and conditions pertinent to the development, implementation and review of a continuing education program; and a projection of some directions for the future.

## DEFINITION

For the purposes of this analysis, continuing education is the generic title being used to refer to the organizational unit or units in a college by any one or more titles such as those listed below, which is responsible for instruction other than the traditional credit program. A continuing education program unit often includes any one or more of the following titles, elements or emphases:

— Community Services
— Extension Programs
— Non-Credit Programs
— Lifelong Learning Programs
— Outreach Programs

— Special Projects
— Off-Campus Credit Programs
— Professional Development Learning Programs
— Evening, Summer or Weekend Programs
— Part-Time Adult Learner Programs, or
— Experiential Learning Programs

From an organizational standpoint, a continuing education administrative unit is any organizational unit through which instructional programs and special projects other than those offered as a part of the traditional instructional program are offered. Programs may be offered on a credit or non-credit basis to adult part-time learners or other special target populations as described by the college. This structural unit definition is offered as providing a framework for the organizational analysis in this chapter. It does not preclude substantive educational definitions of continuing education (Boggs, "Philosophies at Issue", Examining Controversies in Adult Education).

The activities undertaken through such continuing education administrative units may include:

— Analysis of learning needs in a potential learner population
— Identification and analysis of the population in specified geographic areas for market segmentation purposes
— Identification of special expertise of the Full Time Faculty for purposes of offering conferences, workshops, seminars or special courses of instruction
— Educational program development with instructional and learning objectives set in place to satisfy the potential students and the faculty
— Design and implementation of an advertising program (apart from the marketing program steps taken above)
— Financial analysis for program development and implementation and price (fee) setting
— Faculty recruitment and hiring to meet college standards

while ensuring appeal to the public interest
— Implementation with attention to logistics (e.g. possibly
  renting a space and ensuring that all support elements
  such as adequate seating, chalkboards etc. are in place)
— Evaluation (including a program content and financial
  analysis) for purposes of expansion, offering again,
  recommending for integration into another area of the
  college or relinquishing

The organizational or administrative unit definition of
continuing education is based on observation and analysis of
what is occurring in the field. It is not prescriptive. There are
common steps taken by continuing education practitioners.
And there are common program activities which fall into the
set of credit and non-credit instructional and special programs
offered by the college which are other than the traditional
curricula. Based on observation and analysis of these common
steps and activities, the organizational/administrative unit
definition of continuing education is asserted.

This definition is intentionally and open-ended in order to
include any unit which sees itself as being under the
continuing education umbrella according to its college's
definition (which may or may not fit the definition of the
"continuing education field"). Such a definition reflects a lack
of clarity in the charge to such units to fill or meet a well-
defined and clear educational mandate as a part of the mission
of the college. There is opportunity for both the continuing
education leadership in this circumstance to clarify definitions
and enhance impacts.

There is also a lack of clear purpose and therefore some
confusion about mutual expectations between the continuing
education unit and the college. This lack of clarity in purpose is
at the foundation of why there are uncertain expectations for
the performance and impact of the continuing education
organizational unit on the college. It is a clarification of
purpose that is the topic of the next section.

# PURPOSE

Apart from any single institutional financial-need purpose, colleges have entered the continuing education marketplace with a mix of purposes which may or may not be consistent with the educational mission of the institution and may or may not be helpful to strengthening the institution. Some institutional reasons for offering continuing education programs are listed below. An examination and confirmation of purpose using this list for review may be helpful to strengthening a continuing education program or the college as a whole.

The reasons for the development and implementation of continuing education programs vary greatly. Clarifying and prioritizing the purposes will help the college and the continuing education program agree upon and accomplish continuing education goals.

## Continuing Education Organizational Purpose List

A. Community Outreach
1. Increasing access to higher educational opportunity
2. Providing opportunity for community development (growth)
3. Providing for an altruistic interest in the growth of the individual or the growth of selected individuals as a special part of an extended mission for a college. (For example, Wellesley College addresses the educational needs of women learners returning to college.)
4. Enhancing community services (meaning the solving of local problems in part with the aid of educational resources)

B. Curriculum and Instruction
1. Expanding the curriculum:

    — Pilot curriculum efforts
    — "Low-Cost" approaches to new and developing program areas (More acceptable use of part-time faculty)
    — More comprehensive offerings (Content and delivery)

  2. Providing avocational instructional opportunity (stimulating creativity for faculty/faculty renewal)

C. Economic and Financial
  1. Providing financial opportunity for faculty
  2. Developing a financial benefit to the college by generating revenues in excess of expenses
  3. Increasing efficiency of facility use and possibly reducing security problems and plant operation costs

D. Public Relations
  1. Enhancing the image of a college or university in demonstrating a more comprehensive operation (e.g. responding to different age groups)
  2. Responding to local demands with special offerings as a "good neighbor" (therefore a political/public relations purpose) despite the fact that a program offering may even cost the institution to implement the program. (Such "local demand" may be from a geographic, political or other constituency and may address concerns such as community or economic needs, job training needs, or leisure time needs, despite the lack of a connection to the specific educational mission of the institution.)
  3. Providing support to alumni
  4. Strengthening ties with local business or industry

E. Authority Mandates
  1. Responding to state or other authority mandates to offer "continuing education"
  2. Diversifying the student body from an institutional (but not necessarily from a student-interactive) perspective

Any or all of the reasons listed above may be involved in offering a program. Regardless of the purpose(s) for entering a continuing education program, clarifying the institutional reasons for entering and operating the program can help build consensus for expectations. Continuing education personnel may be more likely to produce the desired impact for the college if the institutional purpose(s) is clear and communicated. Confirming the purpose(s), which may have implicitly changed over time, can help build institution-wide support for what may be a key unit of the college. For example, general understanding by faculty and administrators that an important reason for the continuing education program in a given college is to build pilot curricula with special populations as opposed to generating profit to help offset losses due to sagging enrollments from the traditional credit programs may help elicit faculty and administrator support to accomplish such a purpose.

## Discussion of Purpose

An apparent altruism of the 1960s in the United States has given way to greater self awareness and self concern in the 1980s. This apparent value change is reflected in the institutional purposes for continuing education programs. Many continuing education programs are no longer subsidized to have social impact but are charged to develop revenue in excess of balances.

While there have been few developments in higher education which have emerged as the result of only a single cause, many higher education administrators seem to have turned to "Continuing Education" as an institutional panacea for helping to solve financial problems during the past fifteen years. Some institutions established or expanded continuing education programs as a hoped for "cash-cow" which would address pending or existing financial crises. As a process, continuing education offered opportunity for the growth and development of individuals toward the completion of a degree, development of a career skill, or the meeting of some learning objective. There were and are many other factors related to institutional reasons for enrolling students in cost-effective programs. This plethora of reasons for colleges implementing continuing education programs has led to ambiguity for continuing education personnel as well as for the institutional administrators. Some have succeeded in these new organizational undertakings, some have not.

Some community colleges have made no distinction between day and evening courses (whether offered for a twenty-year-old or a forty-year-old student) as being part of a continuing education program. For other colleges, such as private junior colleges which may have formerly offered courses, for example, to women only (typically aged 17-22) between 9:00 a.m. and 3:00 p.m., co-ed courses in extension sites would address new populations for that college and fall under the rubric of continuing education.

By what magic or set of circumstances would one such institution succeed financially and another fail in developing a successful (profit-making) enterprise? Certainly, the mix of factors attracting adult learners to continuing their educations converged in the 1960s and the 1970s, indicating an opportunity for colleges and universities to address "new" non-traditional student markets. Some colleges and universities saw a financial opportunity and others saw altruistic opportunity. Some of the factors affecting decisions to enter the continuing education arena were ideological and altruistic and others were pragmatic. Many institutions in the mid 1970s were facing financial decline and were struggling for financial survival.

Through the middle and the latter part of the 1960s, community colleges were opening at the rate of one per week. The commitment of the persons working in the institutions for individual growth and community problem-solving paralleled a national awareness and conscience at the time. For many individuals, the opportunity to work in the community college represented an opportunity to participate in a type of domestic Peace Corps. Linking educational resources to community problem-solving fell under the rubric of continuing education or community services.

Max Raines, a community college leader in the 1960s and 1970s, implemented a Kellogg Foundation-supported doctoral program to help develop national leadership for the community college "movement." Graduates, presumably, would help develop the community service and continuing education functions of the institution by developing new educational resources or by linking existing educational resources to solving individual and community problems. Skills in community problem-solving and the development of links between the new community colleges and the problems of specific communities were developed as the tools of the community services function. Teaching and learning as the substantive mission of the college, in the broader community on an outreach basis, continued as the educational mission of the college. Traditional classroom experiences with defined instructional strategies limited the creative approaches required to address social problems and educational needs. Many community colleges meanwhile were developing links to communities and opening their doors to a wider and wider segment of adult learners requiring special instructional approaches. This activity incurred expenses.

Economic development, community development, political development, business/industry development and other categorical terms were used to define the community services function of the community college as linking educational resources to community problem-solving. Each category included educational programs which would be developed and delivered in collaboration with the appropriate community partners and interested parties in order to develop, design, and deliver appropriate and effective instructional programs. Typically such instructional programs would involve adult learners. The learners might be low-income neighborhood residents, employees or potential employees, volunteers working to solve a community problem, or others. Instruction might be offered for credit or no credit; in a formal classroom or a storefront; at a business/industry site or at a public service site. The context for the development or packaging for a particular set of learning experiences was to address and solve a particular learning need, individual or community problem. There was little economic press to generate new students. The broader social context was to enhance access to the educationally disenfranchised and to help solve community problems. While grants and state funding formulas provided practical financial support for these expanded continuing education programs, tuition was the main financial support for private institutions whose purposes were different.

Many professionals who had been in "Continuing Education" as a field identified with the community and individual problem-solving approach. Others identified minimally with an aspect which involved adult learners and left the initiative for action with the adult learner to find the educational resource suited to his or her need. The community service approach begins with an initiative in the institution much as the Peace Corps worker or an extension agent of the Land Grant University would function. It proceeds with an educational need analysis involving the potential student. The assumptions that education provides the basis for self-determination and that the community college is responsible for initiating action to provide education for individual and community college to initiate action to provide education for individual and community self-determination underlies the thinking that the institution is responsible for educational needs analysis, and educational program development, implementation and evaluation. The linking of educational resources to educational needs was reinforced as an approach to a fundamental community service/continuing education function of the community college.

For some thinkers and practitioners in the field, the community service approach and function would ideally be eliminated as a special unit as the whole institution would be a community service college. There was an idealism and altruism which characterized the development of the community service/continuing education approach which is fundamentally antipodal to the institutional continuing education purposes aimed at generating new students and new revenues in the 1980s. The transition from one purpose to the other was gradual and perhaps necessary in light of contemporary financial exigencies.

The community services approach of the 1960s provided an outward-looking purpose to service the needs of new clientele as the primary beneficiary of institutional resources. The driving force of the more recent continuing education thrust has been to identify new clientele who may represent new potential FTE reimbursements or new tuitions. The primary beneficiary in this extreme is the college. The former thrust was outwardly motivated for the benefit of the client, the learner. The latter thrust has been motivated by an institutional self-interest. Certainly, if the institution collapsed financially, no educational needs would be addressed by it.

While the shift in the purposes appears nearly dichotomous, the skills of the practitioners as educators and entrepreneurs have been nearly the same. Under the rubric of either thrust, continuing education practitioners have acted to identify and address the learning needs of "new" students. A shift in expectation by college administrators has evolved. Getting clarity on how the two overriding themes can operate without conflict necessitates an identification and confirmation of the continuing education purposes in a college.

Have these two different institutional purposes on the extremes for implementing continuing education programs created confusion in community colleges? Can such purposes operate together?

The success of community colleges in attracting older students with a mission that had been development-oriented certainly appealed to the interest of other higher educational institutional types. First the four-year state colleges, then the major universities, and more recently private higher educational institutions offering educational opportunity to older students has emerged. While some institutions (e.g. Harvard University) have had long-term commitments to offering credit and non-credit instruction to a broad public, other institutions entered the continuing education marketplace as a result of an interest in bolstering sagging enrollments and in order to address the problem of declining coffers. Some institutions, for example, Fisher Junior College, were literally able to save themselves from closing through the financial success of their continuing education operations. Stories of such successes perhaps attracted other institutions with similar financial needs to enter the continuing education marketplace. Parenthetically, some of these latter institutions failed in their continuing education efforts at institutional fiscal salvation.

Clearly, there is no single right reason for all colleges to enter continuing education. There also is no universal reason why an institution cannot extend its mission or change its mission in order to adapt to new challenges (e.g. financial or changing demographics) or to address new needs (e.g. opportunity for Spanish-speaking women in the neighborhood to gain employment skills). In fact, such adaptations are essential. There are compelling organizational reasons however, that the mission of a college be clear and that the component parts of a college complement one another and that there be clarity among the individuals in the college as to the purpose of the continuing education program and its relationship to the college as a whole.

The opportunity to define institutional mission according to what is tried and happens to work (a pragmatic approach) is an interesting approach and perhaps peculiar to private two-year colleges. The application of an entrepreneurial pragmatic principle is a guideline in some settings: "If it works, do it." Hence, a continuing education operation may have been begun for any one or more of the listed reasons and continued because it worked. The reason may not be directly tied to the institution's primary mission. The reason for offering or not offering a program may be whether it returns a profit. Institutional integrity is never questioned within such a framework.

According to this principle, an institution's mission is defined by examining where the college or university commits its budget. There is an approach which suggests that "If continuing education programs generate profit, let's run them." Certainly there would be few individuals/educators/executives who would argue that the commitment of a budget in a program area is evidence of an institution's mission in the practical order of operations. The answer to the question: Were there any revenues or expenses generated for continuing education?, permits an immediate answer to the question of whether continuing education is a mission of the institution for the period in question. It does not clarify the mission of a continuing education organizational unit or of the college to establish one unit whose sole purpose is to generate profit. The educational mission, as such, is absent.

Just as a commitment to single-sex higher educational opportunity in a metropolitan environment for young women of 17 to 24 can drive the development of an educational institution, so too would institutional integrity be assured by entering into continuing education efforts because they are consistent with the purposes of the service-oriented nature of the institution not just because they generate money. Such a commitment hardly precludes generating revenues in excess of costs.

For many institutions, entry into the continuing education marketplace as an approach to solving a financial problem has lacked continuity or clarity in purpose. The continuing education program for many institutions added expenditures in excess of income rather than a profit.

While the continuing education operation of a college may provide excess revenues to college coffers, the charge to the Continuing Education Administration needs to be clear. Moreover, the unit is more likely to be successful if the mission of The Continuing Education Program is fundamentally tied to the mission of the college (e.g. to provide professional educational programs at the technological level while generating a financial surplus).

## FACTORS

There are internal and external factors pertinent to the successful development, implementation or review of continuing education programs. The impact of a continuing education program upon a college and the college's expectations for the continuing education program can be more realistically established if internal and external factors are identified and assessed.

This section of the chapter includes a list and an analysis of some typical internal factors which will assist in factor assessment at specific colleges. The list includes Faculty, Administration and Curriculum Factors followed by a separate discussion of the time and space factors, and finally a general discussion of internal factors.

## List of Internal Factors

There are many factors internal to the operation of a college or university in addition to time and space which may affect the success of a continuing education program. The identification of and accommodation to those factors will help provide the basis for a more effective program. They are outlined below under the categories of Faculty, Administration, and Curriculum with discussion following.

### *FACULTY:*

1. Perception of Continuing Education (Disinterest)
2. Interest (Disinterest) in different (e.g. older, working) kinds of students
3. Interest in developing different instructional approaches
4. Interest in developing different curricula (e.g. to respond to special "continuing education" needs or to develop new programs on a pilot basis)
5. Potential need for faculty development efforts to support continuing education
6. Interest of faculty in developing/supporting adult learner facilitative approaches (e.g. CLEP, Experiential Learning Programs, GED, or Adult Basic Education Programs)

### *ADMINISTRATION:*

1. Understanding of and commitment to the continuing education mission of the college
2. Addressing what may be the conventional wisdom on campus regarding the continuing education experience (e.g. the value of the degree, the course standards, credit vs. non-credit issues and others)
3. Addressing public images of quality education or accessibility for the college as a whole to which continuing education is a part
4. Providing support to overcome barriers (e.g. geographic,

financial) through support for outreach or special financial
aid arrangements

5. Identifying safety and security support needs
6. Providing for ease of transportation/parking
7. Ensuring appropriate student supports for what may be an
   older student population (e.g. childcare, times for
   registration, etc.)
8. Clarity in providing support functions (e. g. registration,
   research, budget, staff) as part of the operation of the
   college or university.

## CURRICULUM:

1. Clarity of relationship between credit or non-credit course
   offerings by Continuing Education and another academic
   unit of the college.
2. Clarity on content of credit course offerings by or through
   continuing education in comparison with or in contrast to
   the same of similar courses offered by another academic
   unit
3. Status of quality and standards issues with respect to
   transferability to another unit of the college, meaning of a
   degree if credits all come from the continuing education
   program, or other value questions
4. Status of CLEP, Experiential Learning, or Independent
   Study Programs from a curricular standpoint

   The internal factors are, as a group, logical necessities for a
continuing education program. There must be faculty,
administration, curriculum (or learning content), and time and
space in which learning/teaching occurs. The absence of any
one of these categories of factors would preclude the
development and implementation of a continuing education
program. The importance of the internal factors to the success
of a continuing education program then cannot be minimized.

## Discussion of Internal Factors

**Faculty** Of faculty factors related to impact on continuing education, perhaps perception is the most important since it affects all of the other faculty factors. To the extent that the full-time faculty perceive the continuing education operation as something "less than," "other than" or "outside" of the college, a significant and influential constituency will be lost as a potential positive force to the continuing education operation. Most continuing education practitioners recognize the need to "bring the faculty along" and have developed strategies such as overload instructional opportunities for additional pay and consulting opportunities to help faculty become knowledgeable, supportive and committed to a quality continuing education program.

There is a corresponding need for academic administrators who lead the faculty to be brought along. The extent to which there is a positive or negative perception of the academic quality of the continuing education operation is a matter of institutional concern for all administrators and faculty.

Full-time faculty interest or lack of interest in dealing with matters of specific concern to continuing education may vary to the extent that individual colleges promote the development of alternate instructional approaches to respond to different student's learning needs. Continuing education students typically represent a unique student population warranting unique instructional strategies. Full-time faculty have special opportunity in continuing education programs to develop such strategies. Some colleges also promote the opportunity to develop new curricula on a pilot basis through the continuing education operation of the college. Faculty interest and a corresponding institutional support of faculty in developing new curricula and new teaching techniques is important to enhancing full-time faculty involvement in continuing education. The continuing education executive needs to take an active leadership role to posture the president or the appropriate academic vice president or dean with the faculty as being supportive of faculty involvement either by load definition or by overload opportunities. The full-time faculty will benefit by the involvement in Continuing Education and the continuing education program will benefit by the involvement of the faculty.

Professional development opportunities to strengthen instructional skills or assessing part-time faculty provide special professional incentives for full-time faculty. It is appropriate that colleges which by definition provide opportunity for individual growth and professional development for students express commitment and program support for faculty as a part of an institutional mission.

College missions vary. So the posture of different colleges vary with respect to either the mission implications or appropriate educational value of programs such as CLEP, Experiential Learning, Independent Study and others will vary. Faculty consideration and appreciation for the appropriateness of some of the above programs warrants the direct attention of continuing education and college administrators. Such unique instructional approaches are typically used in the outreach/extension efforts of continuing education and may reflect alternate instructional (including testing and portfolio development) approaches opposed to alternate curricula.

There have been implications for administrative support throughout the discussion above. Some specific comments below elaborate on the outline of factors under the category of Administration.

**Administration** If the mission of the college or university is clearly stated to include continuing education goals, then the continuing education operation is more likely to meet performance expectations. The highest administrative personnel need to clearly articulate the importance of the continuing education operation as a partner of equal status with other major academic units in the college/university. Unequivocal administrative support for continuing education may help dispel pecking order problems and other institutional blocks to effective program development.

In colleges where credit programs are offered through the continuing education organizational unit, there must be no confusion about the acceptance or meaning of the credit offered and its acceptance in meeting requirements for a degree. Formally, the problem of single college (single academic institution) and single degree-granting institutional authority is the issue. (Questions of licensing authority by whom and to whom can typically be dispelled by examining the appropriate enabling state legislation or state code.) Traditionally, the reliance on entrance requirements to traditional colleges has implied an academic quality and academic process. The typical open-door admissions of continuing education programs has apparently implied a different academic process in working toward a degree. Many faculties have determined that a degree earned through continuing education processes would need to be specified as such. Is there a need to confirm what needs to be common in the curriculum (and co-curriculum) whether in a continuing education traditional university program in order to award the degree of that institution? The institution and learning experience while at the institution allows the awarding of the degrees. To distinguish the degrees based upon the entrance requirement suggests that what occurred for students before entering the institution warrants the awarding of the degree. Administrators and academic leaders need to confront this issue in order to reconcile the core esteem issue.

Administrative expressions of college-wide goals regarding quality and access can be assessed in terms of support for Continuing Education programs which provide access or overcome barriers. Public Relations, safety and security, registration, transportation, parking and student life programs are all part of the mix of support efforts to help ensure an effective program. It is the responsibility of the continuing education executive to identify such support factors and articulate their importance to success while assisting other college administrators to effectively implement such support programs in the context of operating the total college.

Administrative support and leadership need to be assertive and dynamic from both the continuing education operating unit and the college as a whole. The college President, Academic Vice President, Academic Dean and Provost, as well as Deans and Vice Presidents of Student Services and Business and Finance need to embrace specific responsibilities for continuing education operations under the rubric of their respective portfolios in order to maximize a most favorable impact by continuing education on the college.

**Students** From an institutional perspective, students are internal factors once enrolled as learners. They are external factors before being enrolled. An analysis of students is beyond the purview if this chapter. Time and space as factors are discussed below.

**Time** The time of day or evening in which a course or program is offered, the season, or the relative proximity to other events can affect the success or failure of a program. From an institutional standpoint, there may be special supports for security, maintenance or special staff if a course or program is offered at 6:00 a.m., or on a Saturday, or in July. The success of a program in addressing a selected target population may be determined by virtue of the time in which the program is offered. Cuyahoga Community College began "Early Bird" courses for a "Downtown" target population at 6:30 a.m. in the late 1970s. The time of the offering permitted adult learners to meet their classes before going to work at their downtown locations. The continuing education administrative unit not only provided significant educational experiences for learners, but also promoted the reputation of the college as a responsible and caring institution. Institutional support for parking and security was essential to the success of the program and these factors were readily and easily addressed because of the time at which the courses were offered. The target population was going to a downtown location for daily work. Travel time was reduced by leaving for downtown at an earlier hour. Parking and security logistics were minimized which added to the attractiveness of the program.

A program always occurs in time. Clearly, continuing education practitioners are experienced in recognizing the importance of offering and implementing a particular program at a certain time because of the relationship to other factors both internal and external. Just as with time, a continuing education program always occurs "in space." Even if the program delivery system is through television, there are space implications.

**Space** The success of a continuing education program has as much to do with location and space as with time. Building on the preceding example will help make the point. There is nothing inherent in a set of desks lined in rows as a necessary condition to learning. The adult working population going to Early Bird courses in downtown Cleveland met in comfortable seminars/workshop settings. Rooms were arranged with juice and coffee available to complement the attractive features of the seminar setting. The space was appropriate to the time the course was offered.

There is an interdependence among factors. Looking at the time factor without considering the space factor or the relationship among factors may spell the difference between success and failure in a program effort.

A blend of factors must be right for success to ensue. To offer a program at a special time such as 6:30 a.m. may prove ineffective. Naysayers may be quick to point out "we tried that and it didn't work." Only after a review of each of the factors and their interdependence to consider whether there was an adequate accommodation or resource commitment regarding each, may the judgment on the program be made realistically.

A barely minimum commitment may be an inappropriate investment of any resource. The impact of the institutional investment will be on the institution as a whole. Therefore the evaluative questions as to whether the time was good, the space was adequate, the administration was effective, the curriculum was well-developed, the faculty was appropriately prepared, all need to be asked. Certainly, if the space is poor, a program may fail regardless of the time a course is offered. The critical mass concept dictates that an adequate (not a minimum) quantity and quality of resources pertinent to each factor be delivered.

From the perspective of impact on success or failure of a continuing education program and impact of continuing education operation upon the college, time and space implications need to be considered not only on their terms but also with respect to their relationships to other factors. College administrators as well as continuing education administrators need to be aware of the significance of these factors as related to expectations for the overall performance of the continuing education operation of the college and its consequent impact on the college to deliver new students, a source of revenue, or other outcomes.

## SUMMARY

Continuing education programs come in many varieties with much in common and yet much that is distinctive. Their purposes vary as considerably as their definitions, which may lead to confusion and mixed if not conflicting priorities. Their need for relationships with other institutional components is extensive, and their effect back on these factors is often substantial.

What general statements can be made about an area which exhibits such variety and uniqueness? We have seen that continuing education programs with a variety of self-definitions are successful. Likewise, such operations are effective at satisfying myriad goals, serving a variety of purposes. We have seen that there may be tremendous variety in the resources and internal factors of successful programs. We assert therefore, that there is no single prescriptive definition, purpose, or blend of factors which makes one program succeed and another fail. What is critical is not the definition or the purpose itself, but rather the *identification* of a definition, the *achievement of agreement* regarding purpose, and the *clear, unambiguous communication* of support which will reverberate among the institutional constituents. Clarity, Consensus and Communication — these are the qualities which ensure success.

## BIBLIOGRAPHY

Barton, Paul E., *Worklife Transitions: The Adult Learning Connection*, New York: McGraw-Hill Book Co., 1982.

Boggs, David, "Philosophical Issues in Continuing Education" in Griffith, William S. and McClusky, Howard Y., *Examining Controversies in Adult Education*. AEA Handbook Series in Adult Education. San Francisco: Jossey-Bass, 1981.

Brookfield, Stephen D., "Understanding and Facilitating Adult Learning," San Francisco: Jossey-Bass Inc., 1986.

Heermann, Barry, Cheryl Coppeck Enders, Elizabeth Wine, *Serving Lifelong Learners*. New Directions for Community Colleges, Vol. 8, No. 1, San Francisco; Jossey-Bass, 1980.

# FACULTY RENEWAL — A HOLISTIC APPROACH TO FACULTY REVITALIZATION

Audni Miller-Beach

It is no secret that teaching is a demanding occupation. After all, administrators and students alike expect instructors to be well-informed, patient, understanding, energetic and what's more entertaining! Faced with these expectations, how do instructors discover and rediscover excitement in their work? How do faculty maintain or regain their vitality, their energy,

**Audni Miller-Beach** is Executive Director of the Maine Vocational-Technical Institute System. She has been an instructor in a two-year technical college and served as a Research Specialist and Coordinator of Postsecondary Programs for the National Academy of Vocational Education at The National Center for Research in Vocational Education, The Ohio State University. Dr. Miller-Beach has served as a consultant to community and technical colleges throughout the United States, and as Director of Training and Development at Maine National Bank. She is recognized especially for her expertise as a facilitator of the DACUM process for occupational analysis and her work in the development of performance-based training programs. Audni Miller-Beach received her M.A. and Ph.D. degrees from The Ohio State University.

their enthusiasm? This chapter is focused on three aspects of faculty renewal: (1) the need for renewal, (2) the process of renewal as it is described by psychiatrists, philosophers and theologians, and (3) sources of renewal as described by community college faculty.

# THE NEED FOR FACULTY RENEWAL

The establishment of faculty renewal programs in colleges and universities is attributed both to changes occurring in the higher education environment and to the characteristics of teaching as an occupation. First, with regard to environmental changes, declining or stabilizing enrollments have resulted in a steady-state academic job market and less faculty mobility. As a result, faculty who no longer have the option of moving to another college as a means of renewal expect their present institution to provide opportunities for professional development.

A second impetus for faculty renewal is the pressure for accountability. In response to such pressure, colleges and universities are expected to demonstrate a higher degree of efficiency at less cost. Faculty development programs are regarded as a mechanism for increasing an institution's efficiency.

Another condition which has contributed to the establishment of faculty development programs is the influx of non-traditional clientele, including older students, students who are poorly prepared academically, the handicapped, and ethnic minorities. In order to respond effectively to these students, faculty need to acquire new skills and perspectives.

Finally, the development of instructional technology means that faculty need assistance in learning how to use new equipment and a wide variety of instructional resources.

# THE NATURE OF TEACHING
# AS AN OCCUPATION

A look at the research concerning the occupational characteristics of teaching underscores the importance of faculty renewal. First of all, teachers experience a great deal of uncertainty because teaching is an unclear technology (Cohen, March and Olsen). The precise relationships between teaching behaviors and learning outcomes are virtually unknown. Lortie describes teaching as a craft "marked by the absence of concrete models for emulation, unclear lines of influence, multiple and controversial criteria, ambiguity about assessment timing, and instability in the product" (p. 136). Thompson classifies teaching as an intensive technology, a custom technology. The techniques to be applied, i.e. instructional methods, are determined according to the specific requirements of the individual case, i.e., student (pp. 17-18). Thus, the relationships between cause and effect are indeterminate and the application of presumed "causes" (methods) cannot be generically prescribed. As O'Connell and Meeth have observed "there exists no universal definition of good teaching" (p. 8).

The tedium of teaching contributes to instructors' need for renewal. Sarason (1971) and Gehrke (1980) raise the issue of the routine and boredom associated with teaching. Both writers observe that teachers may have difficulty in revealing this aspect of their work. Stereotypically, teachers are expected to create an exciting instructional environment. Not to succeed may be regarded as failure. However, Sarason reports that, according to his discussions with teachers, those who had taught for five years or more were no longer as enthusiastic or excited by their work as they once had been and were considering leaving the profession (pp. 163-164). Sarason also points to the possibility that teachers may attempt to develop a routine which reduces the demand for giving, since they are constantly required to give more than they get (p. 167). In describing psychological discomforts experienced by faculty, several writers have cited the isolation experienced by teachers. Teachers themselves report "isolation" as a "cost" associated with the occupation (Lortie, p. 96). Linquist observes that "colleague support and assistance" are "commodities hard to come by in the privatist world of higher education" (p. 4).

# THE PROCESS OF RENEWAL

For men and women, the need for renewal occurs when they are no longer able to find meaning in their lives. Failure to find meaning results in the loss of vitality, the loss of productive energy. To experience renewal, one must rediscover meaning and purpose. According to the literature, the process of renewal involves the following dimensions:

1. *Acquisition of Self-Knowledge.* Renewal involves identification of particular strengths and weaknesses, illusions, potentialities. The value and the dynamics of relationships with others are evaluated in an attempt to come to terms with the self. An examination of personal career aspirations is usually a significant part of acquiring self-knowledge.
2. *Integration of Polarities.* The realization of personal integrity occurs through a reconciliation of opposing conditions within the self, including rational/emotional, adult/child, good/bad, masculine/feminine, young/old, destruction/creation, and attachment/separateness. In developing persons, the thrust is toward achieving a balanced expression of these qualities.
3. *Qualities Associated with Self-Actualization.* Fully functioning, fully alive persons exhibit the following

characteristics: (1) clearer, more efficient perception of
reality; (2) openness to experience; (3) spontaneity; (4) a real
self, autonomy; (5) transcendence of self; (6) creativeness;
(7) ability to fuse concreteness and abstractness; (8)
democractic character structure; and (9) ability to love.

4. *Self-Transcendence.* Persons who are able to detach
   themselves from the world and experience the world as it is
   on its own terms are renewed through peak experiences, i.e.
   moments of highest happiness and fulfillment. In a state of
   transcendence, the person becomes his authentic self,
   capable of more than he had ever imagined.

5. *Play and playfulness are essential to renewal.* A capacity
   for childlike wonder, inquisitiveness, freshness,
   anticipation, and openness to experience sustain a sense of
   aliveness.

6. *Assimilation of Death.* In order to be truly alive, each
   person must confront the fact of his own mortality. By
   experiencing the despair associated with the confrontation
   of death, man is able to live life more fully, in spite of death.

7. *Possession of Ultimate Concerns.* Man's vitality is
   renewed through his dedication to ultimate concerns, the
   values which give his life meaning and direction, including
   family, work, friends, nation, and institutions.

## INSTRUCTORS' DESCRIPTIONS OF RENEWAL

In order to explore the particular ways in which instructors
experience renewal, the author interviewed community college
instructors. Only the instructors' names are ficticious; their
subject areas, ages and number of years of teaching experience
are as follows:

Megan Wright, Dance, age 31, 7 years teaching experience.
Karen Parks, Life Sciences, age 33, 7 years teaching
experience.

Sean McPherson, Printing, age 36, 7 years teaching experience.

Meredith Lane, Secretarial Science, age 38, 10 years teaching experience.

Kay Liston, Nursing, age 42, 14 years teaching experience.

Arthur Moore, Theatre, age 44, 16 years teaching experience.

Josh Adams, Electronics, age 44, 13 years teaching experience.

Chips Ramsey, Accounting, age 47, 13 years teaching experience.

Joe Patton, Welding, age 56, 17 years teaching experience.

Alicia Allen, English, age 56, 14 years teaching experience.

Zachary Burns, Government, age 56, 16 years teaching experience.

During the conversations, the instructors described those facets of their lives which held the greatest significance for them. Through an analysis and synthesis of these accounts, the author developed a description of the process of renewal. This description is presented according to two perspectives. In order to provide a holistic portrayal of renewal, the first part of the description has been constructed to reflect the predominant themes of the teachers' accounts. Excerpts from these accounts illustrate the themes and give the reader a rich sense of the teachers' experiences. In the second part of the description, the instructors' reflections are examined from the perspectives of the literature concerning man's search for meaning. The result is a description which provides a basis for examining renewal in terms of the experiences of individual persons and, more broadly, in terms of the truths of the human condition.

According to the instructors' descriptions of how they sustained meaning in their lives, they discovered meaning primarily through their relationships with others, through work, and through their own beliefs, or sustaining convictions.

## Relationships with Family

When the instructors spoke of the people who gave significance to their lives, family emerged as the richest source of meaning. For example, as they described the role of the family, the teachers used phrases such as "the single most important thing in my life" and "the most important people." Chips described the importance of his family by saying, "I think that the greatest dimension added to my life is by my family . . . the chief concern is there . . . they come right up there at the top." Sean also spoke with certainty about the significance of his wife and two children, observing that, "My family is the most important thing in my life . . . not work, not my own personal success, but my family." Kay declared that she would not hesitate to resign from her job if her husband were transferred with his company to another city. She said, "I certainly wouldn't give up family for something else, you know, so that I could remain here." Meredith spoke of her family in connection with the difficulty of combining the responsibility of motherhood and career. Meredith related that:

> With the children and the seminars and the working . . . I feel guilty. I think, gee, I'm spreading myself just a little too thin, you know, you do get cranky at home when you shouldn't. I'm crabby a lot of days when I get home. My kids will say, "you must have had a really bad day at school" and I did but I was really nice at school, which is silly . . . I should be nicer at home. They're my family. They should be the most important thing.

The value of family as a source of meaning was evident in the teachers' accounts.

The meaning which characterized family relationships appeared to be associated with certain elements, including love for children, cooperation among family members, encouragement, and acceptance. For example, several instructors conveyed the enjoyment and satisfaction they experienced as parents and grandparents. In his description of

his four sons, Chips said, "[they] keep my wife and I active . . .
we were active with them when they were in high school, and
we still try to stay active with them . . . I have two grandkids,
and so my life is beautiful." Arthur expressed his satisfaction
as a parent with reference to his children's ability to function
as independent thinkers, stating that "irrespective of what
kind of parenting I did, how effective or ineffective it might be
. . . I did get my children to think for themselves, and I consider
that to be extremely important . . . they're critical thinkers."

One instructor related a different sort of parental
satisfaction, a satisfaction which occurred as a result of a
child's ability to change his self-destructive behavior. This
instructor offered the following account:

> (Our) struggles with teenagers have been very
> significant. But this summer we had the joy of seeing our
> twenty-year old married . . . he really has turned his life
> around. He was just strung out on (pot) from tenth grade
> through twelfth and, you know, not the same person at all
> . . . now within one year's time he has become his old self, a
> different person (with) some goals now in his life.

In addition to the satisfaction which they experienced
through the parent-child relationship, the instructors pointed
to the importance of cooperation and encouragement as
characteristics of family relationships. Meredith, who
returned to college after her children were born, described her
relationship with her children, stating:

> . . . we had a very big adjustment to make the first couple of
> years I was going to school. You're not taking care of your
> family, your children, your household duties, you know.
> But now, it was worth it, because my children have been
> raised with a working mother. They know that mother goes
> to school . . . and we have a really good relationship in that
> way. And I think that they respect me . . . I think they're
> proud of me. And that makes me feel good.

Kay spoke of her family in a similar way, noting that her

husband "has been so extremely supportive . . . he's been very helpful. The nights we have meetings, he'll come home from work and start dinner. It's an 'all-together' type thing." Kay's and Meredith's comments revealed an appreciation of their family's ability to adapt to the changes which came as a result of their work outside the home. Josh, Sean, and Arthur also related incidents which illustrate the value of the ability to accept and encourage the development of a spouse. Sean gave his wife a certain amount of credit for her role in his obtaining a graduate degree, observing that "It's [the degree] as much my wife's degree as it is mine, because she made sure the money was there, and the patience." Josh spoke of his family's ability to adjust to any career change he might make. He stated:

> I don't feel in any way limited or trapped in what I'm doing
> — far from it. I feel perfectly free to change whenever I want
> to, and I will receive support from my family . . . I think
> that's probably where a lot of conflict comes in along this
> time for people, when they get to be in their forties and
> they've been in a job for quite a while and they're not sure
> where they're going. But they don't feel free to do
> something else. I do.

Arthur described the significance of his capacity to learn to "appreciate my wife as a human being and to recognize that the expectations I once held for her were not necessarily the expectations she held for herself." The instructors' descriptions of their family relationships suggested that freedom to change was an especially prized element.


## Summary of Instructors' Descriptions

The teachers spoke of their families as quite important resources for the discovery and creation of meaning. As parents, they expressed satisfaction in their children's development. As developing persons in their own right, the instructors recounted the significance of their spouse's encouragement and cooperation. The freedom and capacity for change emerged as especially important elements in the teachers' ability to sustain meaning.

## Relationships with Students

The meaning which the instructors derived from their familial relationships served as a sustaining force in their lives. The teachers' relationships with students also functioned as especially significant sources of meaning. Throughout the instructors' descriptions of their interactions with students, the notion of the instructors' contribution to the development of others emerged as a predominant theme. For example, Arthur described the satisfaction he experienced in this respect when he said:

> The thing that gives meaning to my life professionally is to see students change . . . to begin to think for themselves, the ability to begin to perceive themselves in a different context than when they began their association with me.

It was important to Arthur that he could "touch people's lives not simply in the imparting of specific knowledge, but in a broader way." Like Arthur, Kay spoke of the value of her ability to affect students' lives. She related the following account of a difficult situation in which she strived to serve as a role model for her nursing students:

> Monday, in this hospital, we admitted a ten-year old girl with leukemia. One of the students said "This is the reason I don't like peds [pediatrics]." I had to say that if no one likes that and if no one wanted any part of the sadness or hurt, she [the little girl] wouldn't have anyone to care for her . . . And that's the time when I hope I'm the very best model for the students, to be able to go in [to the little girl] and sit on the edge of the bed and let her cry . . . and say "We want you to go home, too, as soon as you can," and all the while you

have a lump in your throat . . . [but] you go beyond yourself.

While Kay and Arthur regarded their contributions to the students' development as holistic, Sean viewed his contributions as a teacher specifically with regard to the students' employability. He stated, "I'm not here to count the number of students I graduate every April . . . It's the number of kids that end up working, getting a job in printing . . . that means a lot."

Joe contemplated the implications of his work with reference to his students' futures, remarking that:

> Here I work with the people that are going to step off from my classroom into the world of work . . . I can help that man to provide the monies necessary for him to have a happy and successful life, and perhaps to help his children go on.

Josh also cited the recent employment of a student as an occasion for pride:

> I just received word that one of my students obtained a job in local industry, a real good job . . . excellent pay. I've had this student for two years, and he needed a job. He has a family. He worked hard to get his education, and now it's somewhat gratifying to see that he was successful in getting that job.

Finally, with respect to the notion of contribution, as the teachers talked about their students, it became evident that they hoped not only to contribute to the students' development but also to be remembered by the students for their contribution. For example, Chips noted that "It's nice to see where they (the students) are at . . . and see what they have accomplished. They call me on occasion. They still remember me. It's a good feeling."

Students' responses were a major element in the instructors' sense of meaning. The instructors conveyed a certain reliance on the students' enthusiasm as a source of their own enthusiasm. Megan's description illustrates this dependence:

> The students really keep me going . . . they are a lot of fun to

work with, and it's very rewarding. Some days I come in and I really didn't want to get out of bed, or I'm running late. [But] once I get into class, I just forget all about that . . . if I'm feeling really crummy just their enthusiasm and their energy make me feel better. We use each other's energy to keep going.

Alicia gave a similar account of the relationship between the students' excitement and her own:

I was out of school yesterday when you called me. We had a family tragedy over the weekend . . . it was really hard to deal with. And I was feeling like "I just can't go to school. I'm not prepared to teach. I wouldn't know what to say to the students all day." So when I came in today, I thought, "Oh . . . " And I dragged into school and I got to my first class and the students were excited about being there. They all were there, and they were talking away when I walked into the classroom, and I thought, "I should have come to school yesterday. I'd have felt better . . ." That exhilarated me all day.

Meredith drew attention to the particular kind of enthusiasm generated by adult students who were "working people." She said, "I've got all these adults out there, and they're working people . . . They can relate all these experiences they've had, you know, and yet they know they still need some help . . . these people want to know." From a slightly different perspective, Alicia reported her feelings of excitement about teaching adults:

I'm excited about adult students coming back and saying, "I'm dissatisfied with my job, I want something more, I want to learn" . . . that whole excitement, that they're learning plus the feedback to my excitement with learning . . . it really is fun to learn!

The instructors' descriptions of the nature of their excitement and enthusiasm is of particular significance. They characterized these feelings of excitement as feelings of renewal or rejuvenation. Instructors described a physical phenomenon, a feeling having the properties of, or qualities of "exhilaration," a "natural high," a "surge inside." For example, Alicia spoke of the sensation of renewal as "a feeling inside that makes my blood flow faster . . . I feel like I want to move around . . . I feel like smiling." Arthur said, "My energy level increases, I feel more energetic." Kay emphasized that as she experienced the phenomenon, she acquired a heightened sensitivity to a wide range of feelings. She said, "I feel. I don't always feel good. But the fact that I can feel, even hurt, because I am alive . . . is important."

Instructors reported altered physical, emotional, and intellectual states and corresponding changes in their behavior as results of renewal experiences associated with students. For example, Arthur described intellectual stimulation as an outcome: "[then] whatever I'm exposed to triggers ideas in my own mind . . . [and] I bring my enthusiasm back to my colleagues and then more ideas are triggered."

Regarding her response to renewal, Alicia related that "[her]" response is a whole attitudinal change that lasts for awhile. "I mean, it [the attitudinal change] is not toward just that student, but I think 'here's the breakthrough' and I get excited, and my behavior changes, at least for a time."

Meredith spoke of the way she "takes it [the feeling of renewal] home" with her. She said, "You know [I] just kind of glow . . . [I'm] happier . . . I joke around more because I feel better about myself."

Alicia referred to her impulse to share her feelings of renewal with others: "I tend to be 'talky' about things when they excite me . . . I usually tell my office mate immediately if she's in the office when I'm through with class. I say, 'Boy, I really hit it today, I got a student in there, and I didn't have to spell it out . . .' "

As they talked about duration of the effects of renewal, it became apparent that in some instances, the effect lasts for a day as Alicia mentioned, while in other cases, the effect may last for a year. As he described the effects of his annual expedition in the Alaskan wilderness, Chips said, "... it carries me right through [to June]."

According to the instructors' descriptions of the effects of rejuvenating experiences, the phenomenon of renewal was revealed through changes in the instructors' physical, emotional, and intellectual states. Certain behavior changes were also attributed to the phenomenon.

The significance of students as sources of meaning was further illustrated in the investigator's conversations with Megan and Sean. Megan observed that the students were "a source of new ideas." She pointed out that '[they]' just make you see things in a different light and encourage you to keep trying to find different ways of teaching the same thing." Sean, too, noted his appreciation of students' evaluations, remarking, "Our students are extemely honest. They'll tell you if you're doing a good job or not . . . they're very good critics."

## Summary of Student Relationships

Students were highly valued as a source of meaning in the instructors' lives. The teachers' own feelings of vitality were related to the students' demonstrations of vitality. It was through their relationships with students that instructors achieved a sense of having contributed to the development and well-being of others, including succeeding generations. The significance of this sense of contribution is perhaps an allusion to the importance of "living on" through one's works.

# RELATIONSHIPS WITH COLLEAGUES
# AND FRIENDS

Colleagues were regarded as an important source of meaning in the teachers' lives. For example, the instructors appreciated their colleagues as sources of information and other points of view. Sean's observations concerning his experiences in seminars illustrates this aspect of collegial relationships:

> (In seminars) you're working with people, your peers, printing teachers from around the state, and you get to telling war stories and things that happen and better ways of doing things. That's really neat, because . . . you're drawing on hundred of years of teaching experience.

Arthur expressed the importance of his association with colleagues as a source of regeneration. He said:

> I am the kind of person that constantly needs regeneration . . . I have to anticipate that there are going to be opportunities for me to share with colleagues from other institutions and from other situations and participate in workshops and seminars.

Chips spoke of his need for interaction with colleagues so that he could "get somebody else's viewpoint" regarding course content. He explained that:

> I can read it out of textbooks and read it out of periodicals, but I . . . need some sort of interaction (with regard) to what is important and what is unimportant, what we should cover in the classroom, what we shouldn't cover in the classroom.

Megan commented on the value of her association with colleagues in the children's theatre:

> I choreographed a program for the children's theatre. That was a very good experience because of the director and musical director who were very good people. We worked very well together . . . they're artists in their own right.

Colleagues were also valued for their cooperation and

support. For instance, Sean observed that the "spirit of cooperation" among many of the departments at El Vision contributed to everyone's accomplishments. Megan expressed the significance of the faculty's and administrators' support of the dance program. She said, "It's very encouraging when we do a performance and I see (that) faculty or staff came ... that's very supportive to know that they're in the audience."

According to the instructors' descriptions of their relationships with colleagues, the meaning of these relationships was derived from the teachers' shared interests and concerns, the value of learning from each other, and the element of cooperation which characterized collegial relationships. The instructors described their relationships with friends as relationships marked by the qualities of support and acceptance. Meredith's description of her friend provided an illustration of the importance of friends' support: "I have one particular person I love . . . she keeps me going. When I'm 'down' she'll build up my ego . . . she's helped me a lot."

Acceptance was regarded as another important dimension of friendships. Arthur observed that the quality of mutual acceptance was especially significant: "[my] ability to accept the failings of my friends, just as they are willing to accept my shortcomings — that's important to me. That gives meaning to my life."

## Summary of Relationships

Relationships with colleagues provided opportunities to exchange ideas and information, to seek confirmation regarding professional notions and practices. Friendships supplied a different sort of confirmation, the confirmation of personal worth and acceptability.

# WORK AS A SOURCE OF MEANING

As the instructors talked about origins of meaning in their lives, it appeared that relationships were valued for their relative stability and certainty. Instructors spoke of families and friends as important providers of "support" and "encouragement." Students were relied upon as a stable source of the instructors' feeling of contribution. Instructors did not speak of the need for newness or variety in these relationships. By contrast, the teachers cited the opportunity for change and the value of new experiences as the qualities which infused work with meaning. New experiences were almost always described in conjunction with the expansion of instructional programs. Instructors whose programs were expanding were renewed as they developed new courses. Conversely, those instructors whose programs were diminishing in enrollment were frustrated by the absence of the challenges which accompany the teaching of advanced courses and the development of new courses. An illustration of the former, Arthur explained the relationship between the development of a humanities course and his own development:

> I was asked to develop the General Humanities course even though my specific field is theatre. So obviously, I had to seek out materials. I had to develop a syllabus. I had to develop lesson plans . . . that was a difficult embryonic period, so I continued to seek out materials that I thought were relevant. I learned a lot, I learned a great deal . . . (I was) required to read in history . . . in psychology, in areas that I hadn't done a lot of reading in since college.

For several instructors, the development of new courses was meaningful because, as part of the process, they had opportunities to develop relationships with administrators and learn about administrative processes. In this regard, Meredith gave the following account:

> Shorthand is kind of a new program for me. When I came

out here, I had never taught shorthand . . . So for the last two years, I have had to really research the shorthand program . . . and we've ordered a whole new shorthand lab . . . and I had to write up lots of proposals, go to board meetings. Everybody helped me . . . the head of my department helped me, the dean helped me. They went to board meetings with me, to be supportive doing this type of thing.

For Joe, his first series of experiences with the program advisory committee was especially challenging. He said, "Before, what I had to do was to work with the administration. Now I had the administration plus them [the advisory committee], and I had to meet certain standards which the state required." Joe found the committee to be demanding and critical in constructive ways. He recalled that:

"The meetings we held were very frequent in the beginning . . . I would write up my course syllabi and the outlines of the performance exercises . . . and bring them back to the committee and they in turn would tear this thing apart. They would say, 'Well, this sounds good, but we don't like this, throw this out. Add this.' So I found in doing a lot of writing and rewriting that I had designed a program these people [the advisory committee] were satisfied with. So it was quite an experience."

Joe regarded the initial activities in program development as a particularly stimulating phase of his teaching career.

The importance of opportunities to teach advanced courses as well as basic courses emerged as an element in the meaning attributed to work. Alicia talked about this element as she lamented the effects of diminishing enrollments. She said:

If we don't have fourteen or fifteen students, then the class won't go. So if you have only six or eight students . . . that want to feel that additional challenge of reading more literature or whatever, the class won't go . . . Most of our classes don't go, so that the things that used to be fun

courses for me, even though they were a great deal of work,
I don't have anymore.

In a similar vein, Zachary noted the significance of
occasionally "getting to teach" an advanced course:

> I am now teaching a course with seven students in it. It's
> supposed to have a minimum of ten in order to go, but they
> let it go this semester with seven. And my semester, all of it,
> is more pleasant because I have got that to look forward to,
> just something different, something different.

Zachary's and Alicia's observations illustrated the
frustration which several teachers expressed with regard to
teaching the "same basic courses." For example, another
teacher, who said that she "loves teaching," commented that:

> You get to a certain point where you know your subject
> matter very well, and you don't feel like you are really
> growing ... I'm teaching the same thing ... I'm starting all
> over this semester with new kids teaching the same thing. I
> really hate that feeling (of having stopped growing).

Unlike the liberal arts instructors who felt a dearth of
challenges, occupational instructors described the challenges
of keeping up-to-date in their subject areas as a source of
meaning. Straightforwardly, Chips expressed the significance
of "keeping current": " ... as far as the teaching profession, you
either stay current, or you die, I guess . . . and that's about
where you're at." Josh's comments as an electronics instructor
support those of his colleagues in accounting: "What you try to
do, if you want to keep up at all, is apply for every seminar or
meeting or class that comes along and hopefully pick up
enough information so that you can keep abreast." Of his
experiences in this regard during the last twelve years, Josh
observed: "It's like I've been retrained, really, three times in
twelve years." Kay's remarks echoed the others': "There are so
many changes all the time. This summer I went to a workshop
in the field of fetal heart monitoring which is becoming the
'thing' that we have to know about, you know."

## A Sense of Artistry

In addition to talking about challenge and variety as elements which distinguish work as a source of meaning, the instructors spoke of their own sense of artistry as a source of significance. For occupational instructors, this sense was realized in the products, or outcomes, of their trade. For example, Joe described the pride he experienced as a welder:

> In all the courses that I had had, I never found anything that had as much of a challenge as welding has. So anytime I get in the shop and I go ahead and give a demonstration, and when that bead is the way I want it to be, there's a great deal of personal satisfaction in knowing that I can do it now, perhaps, as good or better than I did the day before.

Sean related his satisfaction as a printer:

> Last night's class was a good example. I was showing my photography class how to do some finishing operations on photographs. And I caught a spider web and it was loaded with dew and I shot two rolls of film on it one morning ... and I produced a photograph. It was so neat, and they (the students) were impressed. And I'm very seldom impressed with my own work, but I was impressed with that particular image.

Megan offered the following observation concerning her ability as a choreographer:

> It's just like taking Picasso's paintings when he was just starting out ... and then later on. If you keep working at it, you know it's bound to improve and become more sophisticated and more interesting, and also more of yourself. I think last year ... both dance pieces were really my choreography with very little influence . . . it was interesting to see that, rather than somebody else's variation.

Arthur described his artistic pride as a theatre director, stating, "There's artistic satisfaction in knowing that the production I helped mount on stage is the best possible thing that we can do within the given circumstances." For the instructors, the nature of the craft and their excellence as craftsmen gave meaning to their work.

### Summary of Work as a Source of Meaning

One of the most striking aspects pertaining to work as a source of meaning was the importance assigned to the notion of work-as-process. That is, the instructors found meaning in their work in relation to the opportunities provided for variety, change, challenge, movement. They emphasized the value of developing new programs, teaching advanced courses, and attempting to stay abreast of rapidly-changing technology. Even when the instructors spoke of their pride in creating objects or impressions, the satisfaction seemed to stem from the enjoyment of the creative process as much as from the result.

## SUSTAINING CONVICTIONS AS SOURCES OF MEANINGS

Relationships with family, friends, colleagues, and students, the challenges and possibilities offered in work, and the contrast of nature created a rich repository of meaning for the instructors. They could illustrate these facets of meaning with some effort as they talked. However, the discussion of convictions as sources of meaning were to some degree more elusive and less easily articulated. These convictions included the belief in God, the exercise of intentionality, and confidence in the future.

## Belief in God

A belief in God was discussed in conjunction with the frailty of mankind. For example, Kay stated that "There is a source of strength beyond your own human strength. When you wear out, there's a far greater power to call upon." In expressing her certainty of life after death, Kay maintained that, "I really have that steadfast belief and faith that this life right now is not all there is there is more. There is a heaven . . . "

Sean emphasized the point that he had his own way of addressing the problem of God. In the same sentence, he revealed recognition of the human condition, stating, "You find out you aren't invincible at some age — I believe in God, and it does have an effect on my life. I think it affects the way I approach life. It has to, unless it [the belief] is shallow . . . it's another dimension. As a family, we attend church and that's important to us all."

Through their discussion of the belief in God, instructors revealed regard for their faith as a guiding force in their lives.

## Intentionality

Arthur and Alicia each expressed faith in their own acts of consciousness. Arthur stated:

> Perhaps the most important thing to me is getting in touch with myself as a human being, the changes . . . the awareness that I can control my own feelings, that I can really change whatever behavior seems to be inappropriate . . . I can remember quite distinctly when I hit thirty-seven . . . I began to feel very depressed about myself as an individual and also as a teacher. I had lots of feelings of inadequacy. So there began to take place in my life some very conscious changes. In other words, I decided to do something about that. I made some very conscious decisions over a period of a number of years.

Alicia discussed the fact of multiple realities, saying that her sense of reality was one which:

> encompasses the notions of freedom and responsibility ... I have a sense of reality and the real world is a place where we grapple with ideas. We don't simply have to accept what's out there as real ... what I'm trying to teach is that there are choices and that the choices are not simplistic ... probably ninety percent of our choices are not anywhere near clear ... not good or evil.

The instructors' statements regarding their convictions disclosed various philosophies. Josh's description of his sustaining belief was from another perspective. He attributed his ability to persevere to his plans for the future. Josh said:

> There's a lot of places that I'd like to go and there's some things that I'd like to try doing ... I have a lot of fantasy ideas, like take a boat to the South Seas! But there are some possibilities, like changing careers, real estate or business or engineering go back to industry, or maybe teaching overseas, or something of that nature.

## Summary of Sustaining Convictions

Several instructors revealed their trust in powers they consider greater than themselves. Others emphasized their selectivity and control of their own consciousness. For another, the possibilities he contemplated for the future were a sustaining force.

# ACQUISITION OF SELF-KNOWLEDGE

The literature revealed that renewal involves the person's identification of his particular strengths and weaknesses, illusions, and potentialities. An examination of personal career aspirations, and personal relationships, are significant aspects of acquiring self-knowledge. Accordingly, the instructors' accounts reveal their attempts to discover an appropriate niche for themselves in terms of an occupation. For example, Sean spoke of his decision to leave industry and enter teaching: "I became disillusioned with private industry . . . I decided there must be something better, so I started looking. It took me about a year, and I got the job here [El Vision]." Similarly, Chips described the value of his past experiences as a basis for making choices. He said, "I like teaching . . . I have done other things in my lifetime . . . so I know what I don't want to do . . . but I am real pleased with teaching." Kay spoke of her need to have a career outside the home. She said: "I am a much happier person when I'm outside of those four walls. That goes way back to when the kids were young . . . my husband said, 'I think all that's wrong with you is [that] you should go back to work part-time and see something beyond [home].' I would rather have the satisfaction of teaching than just keeping things polished and scrubbed."

The search for self-knowledge also involves an examination of the person's abilities, illusions, and potentialities. In his discussion of his "mid-life crisis," Arthur described the outcome of his efforts to know himself: "I found out about myself, who I really was, what I really wanted, what my needs really were." As a result, Arthur developed a different sort of relationship with his wife:

> I have learned to appreciate my wife as a human being and to recognize that the expectations that I once held for her were not necessarily expectations she held for herself. I think there's been introduced into our marital relationship a level of compassionate support that perhaps wasn't there earlier on.

With regard to the search for self-knowledge as an element of renewal, the instructors spoke of the search in terms of the choice to enter teaching as an occupation and the satisfaction of having acquired self-knowledge. Arthur's description regarding the change in his marital relationship corresponds with the notion that the acquisition of self-knowledge involves an examination of relationships with others.

## Qualities Associated With Self-Actualization

Of the qualities associated with self-actualization, the ability to love and openness to experience were evident in the instructors' accounts. For example, with regard to an ability to love, the instructors valued their relationships with family, friends, students, and colleagues. Although they did not speak directly of love, the instructors spoke lovingly of the persons who gave meaning to their lives. For example, Chips said "I have two grandkids, and so my life is beautiful." Kay spoke of the care and concern apparent among her friends. She said, "I have a lot of friends . . . we really care about each other." Other instructors regarded their families as the "most important" thing in their lives. The instructors' language and their manner of expression seemed to indicate that they loved and were loved by others.

Openness to experience was another quality of self-actualization which became apparent in the instructors' accounts. For example, Chips described the importance he placed on taking risks with regard to new experiences. He declared, "As doors open, we gotta move. I guess that's what I've been doing all my life; as doors open, I move . . . it may be wrong, but at least you've gotta give it a shot."

Arthur's ability to be open to experience was revealed through his remarks concerning his ability to fully appreciate the "present moment." Arthur said, "One of the things I've learned to do which is extremely important to me is to live in the here and now. That is, I'm enjoying this particular experience because I recognize that when I walk out the door . . .

I may cease to be." Arthur's description of his capacity for living in the present also discloses the recognition of his own mortality.

## PLAY AND PLAYFULNESS

According to the literature, play and playfulness are essential to renewal. In their accounts, the instructors did not reveal the quality of playfulness. However, instructors did speak of play in the sense of "non-work." For example, Chips said, "When I work, I work, when I play, I play." Regarding his annual excursions to Alaska as play, as refreshing escapes from the ordinary, Chips gave the following account:

> I don't teach summers any longer, and I normally fill a duffel bag and go to Alaska for five to eight weeks I just come back when I feel the time is right. But I go up there and do nothing. I take my watch off, don't look at a calendar, don't read a newspaper, don't listen to a radio, don't watch T.V. . . . it's refreshing.

Chips remarked that he had to have a "change of pace" and "escape from people, more or less."

When Josh described those activities he "loved to do," he spoke of them in a manner that implied play. He said,

> I like to fish. But they don't pay much these days! I like to drive my tractor around . . . I have an untold number of jobs waiting for me . . . that I love to do. Cut wood . . . maintain tractors and boats and cars and lots of contraptions . . . I love to read, too, [I do] a lot of reading.

Several instructors related the importance of achieving a balance between work and play. For example, Karen said, "I love having summers off . . . I use a lot of that time to relax. I like to camp, travel around the country. I'm a big sports nut racquetball and tennis. Sports may exhaust me physically, but I think mentally I'm more prepared for everything else."

Karen's comments illustrated the instructors' awareness of the value in pursuing a variety of activities.

## ASSIMILATION OF DEATH

Man's confrontation of his own mortality is also essential to the process of renewal. By experiencing the despair associated with the confrontation of death, man is able to live life more fully, in spite of death.

During their conversations, the instructors did not directly address the subject of their own mortality. However, several instructors described the profound effect of the deaths of persons who were significant to them. For example, one instructor talked about the death of his newborn child, saying,

> It was just devastating. It took both of us at least a year to recover psychologically . . . I guess it took us a year to sort out what is really important. And both of us agreed that it's the family. It's our family. And our marriage is really important.

For this instructor, the death of a child caused him to examine and re-examine his values, to determine what had significance and what did not.

Kay spoke of the death of her nephew in connection with her decision to specialize in maternal and child health. She related,

> Maybe one of the reasons why I'm in maternal and child health would go back to the time when we lost one of my nephews. He was very ill, and they called me to the hospital to 'special' him, and he died. [It was] a helpless feeling . . . you nor the doctor could do anything, not one thing to make a difference.

Like Kay, another instructor whose child died suddenly also described feelings of helplessness and despair. The instructor said,

> It doesn't matter who you talk to. It's impossible for you to

have them ... give you something meaningful ... I've really
got to grope more now than I have ever had to in the past in
order to make my life meaningful. I've found that I have
periods of depression, where I never had them before.

This instructor's despair is reminiscent of Tillich's
statement that man must fully know the anxiety of nonbeing
in order to truly experience being. The meaninglessness and
despair associated with death convey the sense of nonbeing, of
emptiness. According to Lifton, it is this emptiness which
provides a meaningful basis for reordering and renewal.

# ULTIMATE CONCERNS

According to the literature, it is man's ultimate concern, the
meaning which gives meaning to all meanings, that supplies
the answer to the meaning of existence. Work, family, nation,
institutions, and religion were cited as ultimate concerns. The
instructors did not speak of the nation as an ultimate concern.
However, they did portray relationships, work, and religion as
values which had "centering power" for their lives. In this
section, these ultimate concerns are discussed.

### The Role of Relationships in Renewal:
### The Courage to Be as a Part.

It has been recognized that in order to engage in renewal,
man must accept the truths of the human condition. For
example, man must acknowledge and somehow address the
dread of ultimate loneliness. In *The Celebration of Life*,
Norman Cousins describes the nature of the loneliness which
characterizes the human condition:

   The eternal quest of the individual human being is to
   shatter his loneliness. It is this condition that enables
   philosophers and theologians to make common cause with

poets and artists. Loneliness is multi-dimensional. There is
the loneliness of mortality . . . of time that passes too slowly
or too swiftly . . . of inevitable separation . . . of alienation . . .
of aspiration . . . of squandered dreams. There is the
collective loneliness of the species, unable to proclaim its
oneness in a world chained to its tribalisms (pp. 42-43).

Man seeks to assuage his loneliness through participation in
human relationships. According to Tillich, man displays the
"courage to be as a part." Tillich explains that "the self affirms
itself as a participant in the power of a group, of a movement, of
essences, of the power of being as such" (p. 89). From Tillich's
perspective, "Only in the continuous encounter with other
persons does the person become and remain a person" (p. 91).
The universal need for participation in relationships was
revealed by the instructors as they described the significance
of their relationships with family, friends, colleagues, and
students. The support, encouragement, and satisfaction found
in these relationships assured the instructors of their worth as
persons. These relationships were essential elements of the
instructors' self-affirmation.

Keen states, "Having the security of a home is the source of
the psychological strength necessary to undertake an
adventure" (*Apology for Wonder,* p. 17). The instructors
conveyed a certain appreciation for adventure, specifically
with regard to the development of their instructional
programs. In many respects, the instructors spoke of their
opportunities for renewal in conjunction with the expansion of
their programs. Perhaps the apparent stability and
satisfaction which characterized the instructors' relationships
may be considered as one element which contributed to their
ability to seek and pursue new experiences, or adventures, in
the work setting. Throughout their accounts, the instructors
described relationships which fostered their self-acceptance,
their sense of accomplishment, and their pursuit of new
experiences. Through these relationships with others, the

instructors were affirmed in their various roles as spouses, parents, friends, teachers, and colleagues.

## Work: An Extension of The Self

Work is regarded as another medium of self-affirmation, a way of coping with the sense of mortality. In the instructors' discussions of work as a source of meaning, the focus was on the value of work in terms of new experiences, as an expression of the self, and as a vehicle for affecting others' lives. Work was seen as only one arena of life. While the instructors conveyed a sense of conscientiousness concerning the performance of their professional responsibilities, they clearly indicated their respect for a balanced life through involvement with other activities.

The instructors valued work as a process. That is, they ascribed meaning to those facets of their work which were characterized by change. They spoke of the results of their work (whether these were in the form of dances or photographs or welded steel) as sources of artistic satisfaction. Instructors did assign a great deal of significance to the fact that they were able to make positive contributions to the lives of students and their students' families. Perhaps this assignation alludes to the desire for immortality through their works. In any case, for the instructors, work afforded opportunities for creative self-expression and the development of their abilities. In this respect, the instructors; creative involvement in their work may reflect the notions in Tillich's statement that "Spiritual self-affirmation occurs in every moment in which man lives creatively in the various spheres of meaning . . . he affirms himself as receiving and transforming reality creatively" (p. 46).

## Religion: The Value of Wonder

In *Apology for Wonder,* Keen emphasizes that man can enrich the meaning in his own life by approaching the world with a sense of gratitude and wonder. Keen's discussion of gratitude and wonder is useful in developing an appreciation of the significance of both qualities for renewal. He explains that if man is to "keep his spirit alive," he must be grateful for the gift of life and "to be grateful that we are . . . radical self-acceptance and integration require that we accept all that has made us what we are" (p. 207). With regard to the instructors' discussion of their renewal, Kay's gratitude became evident in the remark that, "I love life, and I think it's exciting . . . but there's something beyond life . . . there is a heaven." Arthur revealed what may be termed a "radical self-acceptance" when he expressed satisfaction in his ability to accept himself as a "human being with both [his] strengths and weaknesses."

For the traditional believer, gratitude is expressed in worship. For secular man, gratitude is expressed in celebration centered in "the effort to go the depth of everyday experience, and wonder before the meaning that is given and created in the ambiguous and contingent world in which human consciousness is exiled" (*Apology for Wonder,* p. 210). The instructors' accounts revealed both approaches to the expression of gratitude. Their points of view reflected traditional beliefs as well as the beliefs of secular man. For example, Kay revealed beliefs which she termed "biblical." Her belief in heaven and her faith as she described it may be regarded as traditional. Kay's description of her faith implied a gratitude to God which she expressed in worship. Arthur's and Alicia's statements concerning their faith in their ability to choose and to decide, and generally to exercise control over their lives, revealed a less traditional attitude. Arthur emphasized that "Perhaps the most important thing is getting in touch with myself as a human being . . . the awareness that I can control my own feelings." His statement may exemplify gratitude as it is expressed by secular man in "the effort to go to the depth of everyday experience . . . "

Whether man is religious or irreligious, a central element of renewal is the sense of wonder which "keeps us aware that ours is a holy place" (*Apology for Wonder*, p. 211). Through their anticipation of the future, the desire to pursue new experiences, and through the absence of the jaded or the cynical in their revelations regarding the discovery and creation of meaning, the instructors appeared to have a sense of both gratitude and wonder. Dag Hammarskjold captures the importance of this sense of wonder for renewal: "We die on the day when our lives cease to be illuminated by the steady radiance, renewed daily, of a wonder, the source of which is beyond our reason" (in Ferguson, p. 212).

# CONCLUSIONS

For instructors who are pursuing their own renewal or for administrators who are designing faculty renewal programs, the following conclusions point to potential sources of renewal.

## Events Associated with Renewal

The instructors' descriptions reveal that they were renewed through events which provided opportunities for them to acquire new sensitivities, insights, and abilities. These events included the development of new instructional programs and opportunities to exchange information with colleagues. Instructors also found renewal through events which provided evidence of others' development, such as a student's employment in a particular occupation or his discovery of some aspect of knowledge, or those incidents which reflected the

growth of the instructors' own children. Both the development
of the self and the sense of participation in the development of
others are critical to the process of renewal.

Instructors experienced renewal through events involving
change in environment and activity. Persons may be renewed
by pursuing a variety of activities, including work, sports, and
travel. The process of renewal requires a relative emphasis in
terms of work and play.

## Work and Renewal

Certain aspects of teaching, such as course development and
class discussions and demonstrations, contributed to the
instructors' renewal. Instructors were renewed through work
experiences which challenged their current levels of knowledge
and ability. Their pride as artists and craftsmen was also a
source of renewal. The instructors' relationships with students
gave them a sense of having contributed to the development
and well-being of others. Teaching is a source of renewal to the
extent that it provides a medium for personal and professional
development, craftsmanship and self-expression, and a sense
of contribution to society.

## Relationships and Renewal

Instructors experienced renewal through relationships with
persons who supported their growth. These relationships
provided the encouragement which instructors required in
order to invest themselves in new experiences and
relationships. Relationships which support qualities
associated with renewal are a significant force in the
revitalization of persons.

With regard to their relationships with colleagues,

instructors were renewed through opportunities to acquire and exchange information and ideas pertaining to their subject areas. On the basis of these findings, it is concluded that collegial relationships are of particular value as a source of renewal.

## Clarification of the Sources of Meaning and Renewal

Instructors who were asked to describe their sources of renewal expressed the value of that opportunity to examine their sources of meaning. Several of the instructors experienced a certain "consciousness-raising" effect concerning those aspects of their lives which were meaningful and those which were less meaningful. As a result, it is concluded that persons are renewed (that is, that they rediscover meaning) by examining and clarifying sources of meaning in their lives. The process of meaning clarification is valuable as a source of renewal.

# CREATING A CLIMATE FOR RENEWAL

Psychologists, psychiatrists, and theologians have described the elements or qualities of renewal. Instructors have explained how they are able to renew themselves for the work that is theirs in a highly demanding profession. How can these observations and insights influence faculty development practices in colleges and universities? How can educational institutions foster renewal?

## Developing the Faculty's Capacity
## for Renewal

A person's capacity for renewal depends upon his or her ability to be open to experience, to be spontaneous, to be creative. Colleges and universities can provide opportunities for faculty to concentrate on developing their "renewal abilities." For example, faculty development programs can include sessions designed to help participants acquire insights into themselves as developing individuals. Adults rarely have occasions to focus their energies on expanding their awareness of themselves in relation to their various environments. Such an awareness is a critical element in the process of renewal.

## Providing Opportunities for Renewal

As an initial step toward providing faculty with relevant opportunities for their renewal, colleges and universities can sponsor sessions in which faculty are guided through the experience of identifying their particular sources of meaning, their sources of renewal. In these sessions, faculty are asked to develop thorough responses to the following questions: (1) What is it that gives meaning to your work? (2) How is your feeling of meaning related to persons in your work setting? (3) What is it that gives meaning to your life? That is, what is it that "keeps you going" day after day? (4) How is your feeling of meaning related to persons outside the work setting? (5) What events in your life are related to your feeling of meaning? (6) How are certain events related to your feeling of meaning? (7) To what extent does the college (or university) contribute to meaning in your life? (8) What is it like when you feel especially "alive"?

Faculty members' responses to these questions point to those aspects of their lives that offer them the raw material for their construction of renewal experiences. In describing the people and events that are most meaningful to them, faculty identify for themselves the sources they can draw upon for revitalization. For example, if "family" is an important source of meaning, then the next step is to examine the dynamics of those relationships and the specific ways in which these relationships contribute to the faculty member's personal and professional effectiveness.

Many faculty members are renewed through the feeling that they are part of a larger academic community. Colleges and universities can build upon a sense of community as a source of renewal for faculty by helping them develop relationships with other faculty who share their interests and concerns. It is important that faculty have occasions to describe their institutional culture and the facets of that culture which can contribute to their renewal.

For faculty renewal to be more than just an exciting concept for study and discussion, colleges and universities must demonstrate the same commitment to their faculty that they profess to demonstrate to their students: a commitment to the excitement of lifelong learning. Faculty must experience and re-experience the exhilaration—the fun—that comes from finding new meaning in their lives and in their careers. That is their renewal.

## BIBLIOGRAPHY

Arends, Richard; Hersh, Richard; and Turner, Jack. "In service Education and the Six O'Clock News." *Theory Into Practice* 17 (June 1978): 196-205.

Becker, Ernest. *The Structure of Evil. An Essay on the Unification of the Science of Man.* New York: George Brazillier, Inc. 1968.

Becker, Ernest. *The Denial of Death.* New York: The Free Press, 1973.

Becker, Howard. *Sociological Work.* Chicago: Aldine Publishing Company, 1970.

Cohen, Arthur M., and Brawer, Florence B. *The Two-Year College Instructor Today.* New York: Praeger Publishers, 1977.

Cohen, Michael D.; March, James G.; and Olsen, Johann. "A Garbage Can Model of Organizational Choice." *Administrative Science Quarterly* 17 (1972): 1-25.

Coles, Robert, *Privileged Ones. The Well-Off and the Rich in America.* Volume V of Children of Crisis. Boston: Little, Brown, and Company, 1977.

Coles, Robert. Walker Percy. *An American Search.* Boston: Little, Brown and Company, 1978.

Cousins, Norman. *The Celebration of Life: A Dialogue on Immortality and Infinity.* New York: Harper and Row, 1974.

Dean, John P., and Whyte, William F. "How Do You Know If the Informant Is Telling the Truth?" In *Issues in Participant Observation,* pp. 105-114. Edited by George J. McCall and J.L. Simmons. Reading, Massachusetts: Addison-Wesley Publishing Company, 1969.

Dexter, Lewis A. *Elite and Specialized Interviewing.* Evanston: Northwestern University Press, 1970.

Didion, Joan. *The White Album.* New York: Simon and Schuster, 1979.

Douglas, Jack D., and Johnson, John M. *Existential Sociology.* New York: Cambridge University Press, 1977.

Ferguson, Marilyn. *The Aquarian Conspiracy.* Los Angeles: J.P. Tarcher, Inc., 1980.

Fiske, Marjorie. "Changing Hierarchies of Commitment in Adulthood." In *Themes of Work and Love in Adulthood,* pp. 238-264. Edited by Neil J. Smelser and Erik H. Erikson. Cambridge, Massachusetts: Harvard University Press, 1980.

Fowler, James W. Stages of Faith. *The Psychology of Human Development and the Quest for Meaning.* San Francisco: Harper & Row, Publishers, 1981.

Frankl, Viktor. *Man's Search for Meaning.* Boston: Beacon Press, 1959.

Freire, Paulo. *Pedagogy of the Oppressed.* New York: The Seabury Press, 1970.

Gaff, Jerry G. *Toward Faculty Renewal.* San Francisco: Jossey-Bass, 1975.

Gehrke, Nathalie J. "Renewing Teachers' Enthusiasm: A Professional Dilemma." *Theory Into Practice* 18 (June 1979): 188-193.

Glaser, Barney G. "The Constant Comparative Method of Qualitative Analysis." In *Issues in Participant Observation,* pp. 216-

227. Edited by George J. McCall and J.S. Simmons. Reading, Massachusetts: Addison-Wesley Publishing Company, 1969.

Gould, Roger. "Transformations During Early and Middle Adult Years." In *Themes of Work and Love in Adulthood*, pp. 213-237. Edited by Neil J. Smelser and Erik H. Erikson. Cambridge, Massachusetts: Harvard University Press, 1980.

Hallie, Philip P. "Indirect Communication and Human Existence." In *Restless Adventure. Essays on Contemporary Expressions of Existentialism*, pp. 23-52.

Hammons, James O., and Wallace, Terry H. Smith. *An Assessment of Community College Staff Development Needs in the Northeastern United States*. Center for the Study of Higher Education, The Pennsylania State University, University Park, Pennsylvania, 1976.

Howey, Kenneth, and Joyce, Bruce. "A Data Base for Future Directions in Inservice Education." *Theory Into Practice* 17 (June 1978): 206-211.

Hughes, Everett C. "The Study of Occupations," In *The Sociological Eye: Selected Papers*, pp. 283-297. Chicago: Aldine/Atherton, 1971.

Jaeger, Werner. *Paideia: The Ideals of Greek Culture*. Volumes I and II. New York: Oxford University Press, 1945.

Keen, Sam. *Apology for Wonder*. New York: Harper & Row, 1969.

Keen, Sam. *To a Dancing God*. New York: Harper & Row, 1970.

Keen, Sam. *Beginnings Without End*. New York: Harper & Row, 1975.

Kuhn, Thomas. *The Structure of Scientific Revolutions*. Chicago: University of Chicago Press, 1970.

Levinson, Daniel J.; Darrow, Charlotte N.; Klein, Edward B.; Levinson, Maria H.; and McKee, Braxton. *The Seasons of a Man's Life*. New York: Ballantine Books. 1979.

Lifton, Robert Jay. *The Life of the Self*. New York: Simon and Schuster, 1976.

Lindquist, Jack. "The Challenge to Professional Development," *AAHE Bulletin*, September 1980, 3-7.

Lofland, John. *Analyzing Social Settings*. Belmont, California: Wadsworth Publishing Company, 1971.

London, Howard B. *The Culture of a Community College*. New York: Praeger Publishers, 1978.

Lortie, Dan C. School-Teacher. *A Sociological Study*. Chicago: The University of Chicago Press, 1975.

Maslow, A.H. *The Farther Reaches of Human Nature*. New York: Penguin Books, 1971.

Maslow, A.H. *Toward a Psychology of Being*. New York: D. Van Nostrand, 1962.

Mezirow, Jack. "Perspective Transformation." *Adult Education* 28 (1978), 100-110.

Monette, Maurice. "Need Assessment: A Critique of Philosophical Assumptions." *Adult Education* 29 (1979), 83-95.

Montagu, Ashley. "Don't Be Adultish!" *Psychology Today,* August, 1977, 48-50, 55.

Norton, David L. *Personal Destinies. A Philosophy of Ethical Individualism.* Princeton, New Jersey: Princeton University Press, 1976.

O'Connell, William R., and Meeth, L. Richard. *Evaluating Teaching Improvement Programs.* New Rochelle, New York: Change Magazine Press, 1978.

Patton, Michael Q. *Qualitative Evaluation Methods.* Sage Publications, 1980.

Rist, Ray C. "On the Relations Among Educational Research Paradigms: From Disdain to Detente." *Anthropology and Education Quarterly* 8 (May 1977): 42-49.

Rogers, Carl R. *On Becoming a Person.* Boston: Houghton Mifflin, 1961.

Sarason, Seymour B. *The Culture of the School and the Problem of Change.* Boston: Allyn and Bacon, Inc., 1971.

Schatzman, Leonard, and Strauss, Anselm L. *Field Research. Strategies for a Natural Sociology.* Englewood Cliffs, New Jersey: Prentice-Hall, Inc., 1973.

Shannon, William H. *Thomas Merton's Dark Path, The Inner Experience of a Contemplative.* New York: Farrar, Straus, Giroux, 1981.

Smith, Albert B. *Staff Development Practices in U.S. Community Colleges.* Lexington, Kentucky: AACJC, and the National Council for Staff Development, 1980.

Stake, Robert E. "The Case Study Method in Social Inquiry." *Educational Researcher,* 1978, 7 (Feb.) 5-8.

Stegner, Wallace. "The Writer and the Concept of Adulthood." *Daedalus,* Fall 1976, 39-48.

Thompson, James D. *Organizations in Action.* New York: McGraw-Hill, 1967.

Tillich, Paul. *The Courage To Be.* New Haven, Connecticut: Yale University Press, 1952.

True, Michael. "Confessions of a College Teacher at Mid-Career." *The Chronicle of Higher Education,* February 5, 1979.

Wise, Arthur, E. *Legislated Learning. The Brueaucratization of the American Classroom.* Berkeley: University of California Press, 1979.